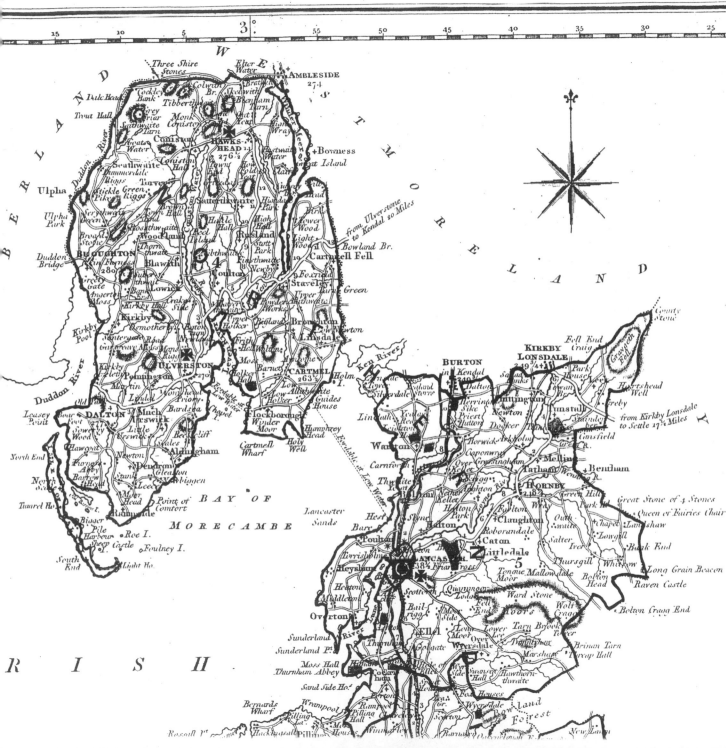

LANCASHIRE.

EXPLANATION.

Market Towns with the distance from London in measured Miles as .... } ROCH 197

Churches and Chapels ....

Turnpike Roads .... Mail Coa.

Bye Roads ....

Navigable Canals ....

Rivers ....

Seats of the Nobility and Gentry ....

N.B. The figures on the Turnpike Roads shew the distance in measured Miles between the Towns.

Railways ....

Population N.th Div.n 343,373 Assesd Taxes £.

D.o S.th Div.n 993,119 D.o D.o £.

9781855624474

CONTENTS

PART I

HALE

We used to visit Hale because of its associations with nearby Speke Hall and the famous giant the Child of Hale. The hall is one of those superb manifestations of the Elizabethan black and white manor houses, all timber and plaster, priest holes galore and a fascinating history as family home. The giant was a Jacobean freak of the 1600s, reckoned to be over 9 feet and equally powerful in wrestling.

Hale village is usually awash with expensive cars, lovingly tended gardens and those picture book cottages and houses that have long marked it out as a desirable residential place: but oh dear ! the nearby airport and the vast modern industrial complexes somewhat reduce its aluring reputation, and it is a village cut off from the country on a sort of promontory with urban gloom right to its doors.

FARNWORTH (NEAR WIDNES)

Between industrial blight and extensive housing estates sits what is left of the old village of Farnworth,

known for its associations with the long gone Bold family and Bold Hall, but still with some nice old properties and above all the medieval church.

RAINHILL

My uncle lived for years in this busy residential district by Prescot, and infuriated my mother by referring constantly to its teeming district as "the village" ! Which is of course what it once was, the spot where William Huskisson, the prominent cabinet minister was run over by one of the very first ever trains, and where the Stephenson's Rocket won the rail race in 1829. One of its claims to fame is the RC monastery and its former resident, Gerard Manley Hopkins, the tortured soul of Victorian poetry.

A village in some respects perhaps ! But the traffic ! and the enormous numbers of 20th century houses too !

KNOWSLEY

The enormous parkland setting of this estate village shields the big house from the swathes of new roads, housing and industrial development which have marked the progress of the century here. This is the ancestral home of the Stanleys, earls of Derby, and with many famous names in their ranks : including the earl

who brought on Benjamin Disraeli as his second in
command in mid Victorian times, when prime minister,
the member of the family who so royally entertained the
Elizabethan court, including the unknown Shakespeare
(all but certainly), and the member who carried the day
after changing sides at Bosworth in favour of Henry VII.
The Stanleys had vast Lancastrian and Cheshire estates
as well as wealth from coal and trade, and led a
reasonably splendid lifestyle for centuries. The hall
is enormous, a sort of composite building from several
centuries of growth.

The park is a vast wild life reserve or game
park, and we used to view the dolphins too at their
sport. My grandmother's great pal was agent to one
earl, and on our visits to see him we would sneak a
view at the great house and at anyone who happened to
be visiting !

CRANK

A sort of moss cum   waste on rising land
beyond St Helens, where scattered brick cottages and
farms still attract renovating yuppies. My father used to
drive out at weekends, dig up some of the wealth of
peat, and rush off quickly - even though, as he said,
it did not belong to anyone !

RAINFORD

My uncle and his family moved here from
Rainhill some years ago, and this former quite small,

south Lancs village has now grown into a vast overflow
of commuter estates all centred on the quite picturesque
village centre of church and shops and cottages.
Plenty of walks add variety, with Billinge rising behind
and Liverpool in the distance.

ECCLESTON

As a child I was brought up on the edge of
St Helens, all fields with a few roads of houses, but
gradually this desirable district has changed into a
vast sea of housing for the needs of the industries of
the towns. Still desirable, and with odd old corners
left including farmhouses and halls, and with the
modern Methodist church we attended, plus the parish
church and its accommodating graveyard. This parish was
an old one which was gradually taken over by its little
chapelry neighbour of St Helen.

BILLINGE

We used to walk the dogs twice a week along the
several paths which skirt still round the farming edge of
this residential district between St Helens and Wigan,
famed for its Lump or hill complete with watch tower
remnant and a quarry which always seemed to threaten to
engulf the hill. Nice woods, fields, excellent views
to the Pennines and across the Lancashire Plain to
Southport; plenty of old farms and cottages, scores of
new developments.

Billinge remains a favoured residential area:
interesting medieval cum classical church too, plus
several smaller old halls (including one with really
spooky grounds and millpond where we trespassed as lads
both appalled at the prospect of ghosts and thrilled at
skulking successfully in forbidden domains !).

DIDSBURY

Once upon a time the village in the southern
tip of Lancashire where it digs deep into Cheshire,
Didsbury village has grown inexorably into a great
suburban part of the Manchester conurbation: people do
say that it retains its villagey flavour ! Pleasant
old village centre with some old properties including
cottages, parsonage and Jacobean church, but rather more
earlier 19th century buildings as the leisured and
wealthy left Manchester for greener fields.

FORMBY

We used to enjoy the total freedom offered
by Formby's enormous sand dune and wooded district by
the shore, haunt of youths and girls as well as rare
toads , squirrels and snakes, and all just up the road
from Liverpool ! The village was once a typical
Lancashire coastal fishing village, but when Southport
was being transformed into a resort c1800, so Formby
commenced its growth into the favoured residential

suburb it is today. Masses of Victorian and later
growth should not mask the old cottages and houses,
usually of nice red brick, and the old manor house of
the 1600s or the parish church of vaguely classical
lines and again in brick. All terribly middle class now
but once a proper working village with thorough mix of
classes and occupations according to my directories.

BURSCOUGH

One of our frequently visited places for
weekend jaunts in the car was Burscough, with a reasonably
downmarket c1830 parish church and miniscule ruins of
the Augustinian priory which was a favoured burial and
worship place of the earls of Derby.

LATHOM

Now known for its enormous modern glass research
laboratories for Pilkington Glass, Lathom retains its
rural feel thanks to the super little c1500 chapel which
we visited every Easter to enjoy the spring flowers and
the scents therein. Pretty almshouses next door, and
over the road the remaining enormous service wing of the
vast Stanley, earl of Derby, hall of c1730 which was
simply demolished. A truly great house which replaced
one of the principal fortified places of the county,
in use to good effect for the king in the 1640s.

ECCLESTON (near CHORLEY)

One of our regular trips was out to this
village spread along a bending main road, with some
good looking brick houses and cottages, a pleasant
parish church set by the little river Yarrow, and
invariably quiet at weekends. The church combined
Victorian with Georgian and medieval: down the road
was its rival RC building, so common in Lancashire.

LEES

This is one of the Pennine mill villages, a
suitable setting for so many TV series and films, with
mills, hills and lots of terraced, grey stone,
properties reaching up the gradients.

HIGH CROMPTON

Old mill and industrial settlement between
Oldham and Rochdale , rather like the previous village of
Lees and with extensive modern growth that belies its
modest c1800 size. Spectacular views and scenery.

HURST

Once also a small rural settlement at the back of

Manchester, Hurst too was suddenly in the forefront of
19th century mill industrial development and was soon
a big village for the manufacturers' workers. Today it
has gone into the rest of the conurbation.

TURTON

In the hills above Bolton is Turton, a place of
more than usual interest since it possesses a whole
clutch of Anglican and Dissenting places of worship,
old industrial premises, lots of lesser old houses,
and links with the Chetham whose fortune created the
illustrious Manchester school. It also has Turton
Tower, an intriguing L shaped house with medieval pele
tower origins, Elizabethan development and later work to
create a combined stone and timber property of great
attractiveness.

SCARISBRICK

Famous for its great hall, Scarisbrick was
well known to us since my cousin went to school there
in the 1960s: the village stretches greatly beyond its
old c1800 confines thanks to Victorian and modern
encroachments, and has the main road traffic pouring
through on the way to Southport. Old cottages and
farms, pubs and shops, but nothing interesting in the
way of churches: but the hall is famous as an early job
of the masterful A W N Pugin, transforming what had been
an Elizabethan hall with 1800s alterations into a daring

essay of Pugin's Gothic work (seen at its best not that long after in the new houses of parliament). What an exterior and interior ! - all panelling, fireplaces, chimneys, mullions, and lavish excess of craftsmanship. Nice grounds too with trees screening all.

RUFFORD

Rufford is famed for its superb hall of the illustrious black and white Lancastrian sort, once so universal, now reduced to a handfull. Its heart is late 15th century, or early Tudor, with various substantial alterations in the 17th and 19th centuries, and all now looking a splendid whole of black and white, with long treelined walk down to the church and village. The village core is brick and the buildings including the grim little church of last century, hardly bear comparison with the hall: good walks in the parkland, by the canal, and in the old days freedom to wander about at will and to enjoy the interior - until crooks started abusing the freedom !

CHURCHTOWN

Now snowed under with new development from both Preston and Southport direction, Churchtown is one of those magical places one recalls in afterlife from one's youth: village centre (despite the traffic), two venerable old inns or pubs, rows of intriguing little

cottages, grander houses, charming 18th century church of St Cuthbert, fine 17th and 18th century hall, and above all the Botanic Gardens. We used to spend several days each year hereabouts, having exhausted the food and entertainment of Southport's Lord Street area, and complete with dogs and grannies, retired to the perfect setting for a warm day. The village is of course utterly urban, but the village feel remains strong and locals still call it that. One of my favourite places to this day.

BANKS

On the way out to Preston from Southport is this once remote coastal settlement, now with much modern growth nearby but still isolated in the depths of a cold season. Most of the coast was like this into the 19th century.

PARBOLD

One of our favourite dogwalks was up the great steep hill that is Parbold, to the socalled beacon, and to run down the far side. It is an invigorating and fresh place though expensive houses now dot about its slopes amongst the trees. Two fine aspiring churches, one RC the other Anglican, grace its slopes too, along with the village of old stone properties and the hall of Georgian vintage: all terribly picturesque,

and complete with farm that provided such ample teas all year round (and a friendly farmer here allowed me to use his ample acres for learning to shoot !). The gents toilet was a wooden enclosure against the pig sty wall , the effluent running out to the stream well below: the ladies toilet WAS a pig sty, suitably equipped for its new customers !

RIVINGTON

Known for its high Pike or hill which we used to look at from our bedrooms to see its high and well lit masts, Rivington also has the extensive Liverpool reservoir and the lovely parkland laid out by Lord Leverhulme for his country home near his roots. Fascinating gardens and old hall, ancient buildings all over the place, and an interesting stone village with its c1700 Unitarian chapel.

T H Mawson was employed widely in the country to landscape and design - his Lancashire and lake district roots centred him on this region, and here working for the soap millionaire he did a lovely job. Interesting little parish church too.

HAIGH

The magnificent late Georgian hall has enjoyed resurgence of new life in recent years. It is out of Wigan that the great Haigh estate of the earls of

Crawford and Balcarres was created, a half way stop for the noble family at their great hall between the Ayrshire HQ and the attractions of London. The hall is big, plain and late classical, used for functions and similar does today, and with superb parkland estate which has been recently put to good use for a variety of recreations and occupations.

The village is an estate one, now encroached upon by Wigan, but with such delightful corners as old foundry, fishpond and 1830s church.

UPHOLLAND

This century has turned the village into a sea of housing and industrial development close to Skelmersdale new town, but along with odd old halls, cottages, farmhouses and corners of what was the village, there is the lovely church, now parochial, but once monastic. This was the Benedictine priory of St Thomas. It was not a distinguished house, though its chancel survives as the main portion of the Victorian church - quite a star turn really for this district.

WYCOLLER

Village in remotest Pennine Lancashire is Wycoller, on back roads to the utterly remote Forest of

Trawdon and at the foot of fine hills. The little stone settlement has links with the Bronte sisters, who lived only a few miles away over the county boundary, and who set their novels in scenery such as this.

DOWNHAM

Wild hillsides and steeply sided valleys are characteristic of this Pennine district, haunt of the famous Lancashire witches in the Jacobean era c1610, and of Harrison Ainsworth's flights of fancy 350 years later ! Downham is always quiet, almost deserted, to look at, but very pretty for all that. The church has a medieval tower but the remainder is 1900s; the hall is a medieval place suitably rebuilt, extended and remodelled for the Assheton family and finally given its front by Webster of Kendal in true classical style.

A place to dwell in summer: Pendle Hill rises dramatically above the village to 1800 feet, and we once went there on Hallowe'en along with scores of others who fancied evoking the spirits of the place ! That is what students used to do, anyway !

CHATBURN

A second Lancashire witches stronghold in the popular imagination is Chatburn, but since Clitheroe is next door, and the main Ribble valley road goes by, it

is rather less remote or evocative of the past - still has plenty of nice old stone houses and cottages.

SAMLESBURY

My father used to fish for salmon and trout close to this former small settlement along the Ribble valley east of Preston - I used to spend hours clambering through overgrown river banks and across deserted woods packed with wildlife, then my chief interest. The hall is magnificent, one of the finest timber framed, black and white halls in a county of fine halls. It seems mostly to be 15th and 16th centuries though with later work too, and the interior with its wealth of period furnishings is fascinating. Really well worth seeing.

Busy traffic all about does not enhance the settlement, something of an estate place of farms and cottages, and a pleasant medieval church plus the inevitable RC rival.

GRIMSARGH

Now too close to Preston's orbit, Grimsargh does not have much to detain the tourist: its church and

housing are 99% modern, though there is one lovely brass
that survived into the new church. Up past here are
several interesting back roads with those enormous
Victorian houses - in one I had to lead a conference,
and it occurred to me that the impossibility of heating
so vast a place must have taken away any pleasure offered
by the views over the Ribble.

GOOSNARGH

       An inspiring village which has attracted
substantial modern growth thanks to its picturesque
qualities and proximity to Preston and the M6. We
used to frequent the pub here, which sits neatly in the
centre close to an old church of various dates, and to
the well known old Bushell Hospital - one of those
early Georgian foundations for the elderly and needy,
and with a handsome range of buildings.

       Out of the village, and the countryside
climbing up to the Pennines is dotted with big houses:
a friend of mine took me to see one being considered by
her wealthy father, and there as an impressionable pair
of students we were staggered by the size and scale of
the gamekeeper's gibbet !

       Memories of country life !

SWILLBROOK

     This rural spot sits over the Lancaster canal,

and it was here that for some years we would pick up
our pleasure craft for touring each May along this
splendid canal from here north to Borwick and
Tewitfield   The bonus of course was that it was
quiet AND had no locks ! (though several nasty little
bridges !)

       The little settlement is made up of modern
developments, old cottages and farms of brick, plus
the canal side properties including the vital supply
shop ! Below Swillbrook was a good pub for the final
overnight stay, and beyond there, the great unknown to
Preston and the main waterway system.

WOODPLUMPTON

       Rather grown large thanks to being a desirable
rural enclave close to Preston, Woodplumpton retains its
villagey feel and   displays interesting old dwellings
as well as a delightful medieval and 18th century parish
church.

RIBCHESTER

       Us locals would drive to this Ribble valley
settlement to visit the famed White Bull hostelry, where
one was sure of fine fare and warm welcome. The most

discerning   of travellers will visit the several
18th century inns and shops, admire the many stone
17th and 18th century properties, enjoy the walking, and
drink in the views across the river valley from the
churchyard: the church itself sits in the site of the
important Roman fort - much information has come to
light about it.

The church is a lovely medieval one with
furnishings from that era and later centuries creating
a homely feel.

DINKLEY

East of Ribchester over the Ribble is Dinkley,
complete with cottages, farms and place of worship:
we used to come for the famed riverside walks and above
all the fishing , and the woods are beautiful.

BROUGHTON

The main road north used to be the much clogged
M6, and the village of Broughton north of Preston grew
along it to service the needs of travellers and the
rural district. Today, despite the M6, it remains very
busy here, and the place is awash with garden centres cum
hotels cum garages cum housing estates. The village core

spread along the narrow road to Goosnargh, now with some
desirable properties.   The parish church is a mixture of
medieval remnant with 19th and 20th century rebuilding.

BARTON

This old village has suffered the same expanding
fate as its neighbours and is now a commuter place.
Odd old halls, cottages and farms have survived modern
times but you have to search them out for your own
interest - they seem to prefer to stay hidden from the
20th century traffic !

CHIPPING

A charming larger village high up on the
steeply rising land close to the river Hodder valley
and other streams that add greatly to the landscape's
beauty. The sort of place that seems to be increasingly
desirable either for retirement or holiday escape,
Chipping has several streets almost wholly of local stone
and forming the type of townscape used in many period
films and TV series.

Little back alleys, entries, lanes and courtyards
remain to be explored and enjoyed, with many dating from
the 17th and 18th centuries. It is a real rural community
too, with plenty of small businesses adding to the

environment and keeping all to scale. Interesting
medieval parish church, links with the Wesley brothers
in the 18th century, and of course a considerable
RC community complete with classical, plain, church
and buildings.

CATTERALL

You turn off the A6 to detour through this
expanding suburban village, close to the M6 and the
Lancaster canal north of Preston and on the road to
Garstang. Not much to detain the tourist, but just a
pleasant community place.

CLAUGHTON ON BROCK

As with so many Lancashire places, Claughton
is best known for its Roman Catholic community and
retains its classically inspired, pre-Victorian, church.
Several old properties of size as well as many newer
ones, and the pretty little river Brock coming close
by - one of the places we used to swim as students, in
hot weather.

INGLEWHITE

On the slopes of Beacon Fell is the village of
Inglewhite, and interesting little stone built place
when I knew it, with a vigorous Dissenting history and
Nonconformist place of worship. Lovely views from it
down to the Fylde.

FRECKLETON

Next to an airport and between Preston and
the Blackpool conurbation is Freckleton, today a much
expanded village with masses of new housing and firms
in a very flat, sometimes quite depressing landscape.
Lack of good building stone meant brick was commonly
used, as here with the church - though in fact the
building is less interesting than its furnishings.

THE SINGLETONS

Great and Little Singleton are modern growth
points for people working in and around the increasing
Blackpool conurbation. The river Wyre flows by and
shows a broad, attractive front for the older brick
properties that remain - though so much here that is
"old" is in fact simply Victorian.

GREAT ECCLESTON

The village today is bypassed by a very busy
main road, but when we first knew the place it was
far quieter and really a pleasant little place - lots of
modern growth too.

OUT RAWCLIFFE

My uncle's father in law was in charge of the
church as incumbent for many years at this quite remote
spot alongside the Wyre river. The church is a very
severe, austere place of the earlier 19th century,
and not at all picturesque !

ELSWICK

For a long time this was something of an
estate village with manor house, but as usual for a
Lancastrian village, modern housing and commuting have
transformed the place.

RIBBY

One of the lesser centres of the Fylde, and
not even appearing on many maps under this name. Yet
it has its older brick houses and cottages, manor
house or hall and parish church in typical Fylde
pattern.

GREAT PLUMPTON

The chief interest of this modern village
lies in its having one of those RC churches by E W
Pugin, somewhat characterless in the way things tended
to be in the mid Victorian years, and a universe away
from his talented Daddy A W.

HAMBLETON

IN a lonely, flat and coastal type landscape
across the Wyre is Hambleton, reached from the
Blackpool end by a toll road last time I was there.
Not a lot to detain anyone historically minded up this
side, though the Fylde countryside has its own rewards
if you like this sort of scenery.

KNOTT END

One of my friends from student days settled into a new bungalow beside the minor road that goes into this remote village close to the north Fylde coast, with an eccentric ferry across the Wyre giving pedestrian access to Fleetwood and Blackpool - by vehicles you have a 12 or 15 mile journey ! The church is one of Paley and Austin's 1890s designs, and all in brick; Parrox hall used to be the place everyone wanted to see, an excellent example of 16th century classical endeavour.

It all seems to be bungalows round this area, the principal contribution to the Fylde architectural landscape this century ! A lovely village in sunny weather but utterly isolated in bad weather.

PILLING

Turn off the main coast road and into Pilling, in flat coastal scenery. The chief interest of the village is in its twin churches, one a fine 18th century building, the other a noted example of the work of Paley and Austin of Lancaster.

COCKERHAM

We used to ride through this village on our horses for longer hacks, then turn right and onto the inviting and extensive marshy coastline that allowed long canters and gallops with frequent falls on treacherous ground. I always got the biggest horse, being reasonably enormous, which meant falls from 18 hands up knocked the wind out of both of us !

The village is a pleasant blend of older properties and modern ones, with several old halls and farms nearby and yet another of Paley and Austin's churches.

Out on the marsh is the splendid chapter house from the abbey of Premonstratensian canons founded in the Norman period: apart from odd stones nothing else in this windswept spot remains, and I suppose that local landowners thought the stone very handy for their houses.   A lonely place at any time, but with the sort of haunting beauty found on the Essex marshes. You can also get away from it all here !

WINMARLEIGH

We used to walk miles, often in wellies, round the country lanes of Winmarleigh when there was no need to speed along the canal. J W Patten, Lord Winmarleigh, would approve of his mansion being an agricultural training college today: he was a progressive landlord, holder of several early Victorian cabinet posts, exceptionally broad minded , very popular, and appalled at the idea that MPs should

have to canvass for support or fight elections - he
preferred gentlemanly agreements ! He also helped out
his pal, the prime minister, by being secretary of state
for Ireland on the understanding it meant not going to
that place !   A lovely and interesting man.

        Good looking church too in the parish.

FORTON

        An old hamlet divided by the 18th century route
of the A6 between Garstang and Lancaster, and made up
of the usual cottages and farms, a few larger old houses,
and modern developments including the one on which we
lived for a year as students. A web of narrow lanes
provided interesting walks including one by the stretch
of canal complete with Georgian bargee cottages; there
is also one of the illustrious Richard Gillow's homes
here (was this the one occupied by the famous singer
Count John MacCormack too ?).

SCORTON

        The M6 skirts right by this pretty little
place, with Paley and Austin's aspiring steeple for the

parish church close to the 6 lane carriageway. We used
to spend winter teatimes in the cafe in the village
centre: delightful ranges of brick properties of all
types and farm outbuildings, and some most desirable
houses.

DOLPHINHOLME

        On the climbing slopes up the river Wyre
district to the Abbeystead reservoir is Dolphinholme,
complete with its typical , classical, hall, its estate
cottages and houses, and the parish church (designed,
with a certain inevitability in this district, by
Paley and Austin in the 1890s). Charming village
from the point of view of looks and atmosphere,
but the countryside is the star with lovely views.

ABBEYSTEAD

        The village is a clear estate one, properly
and carefully built for the earls of Sefton and mainly
looking Victorian like the big house (really a sort of
hunting lodge used by the earls when grouse shooting
was so fashionable). We used to trespass (in error)
through the wooded landscape simply to enjoy the views:
thickly wooded and enormous hunting landscape and estate,

nowadays in the distinctly caring hands of the duke of Westminster.   Interesting Georgian church too.

ELLEL

From the canalside towpath and walks we would look out for the distinctive Italianate towers and decorations of Ellel Grange, one of the great houses of the district and an earlier Victorian effort at making a country house for a discerning businessman.   Lovely wooded grounds marked it out.   In the parkland is the house's chapel, a considerable building of the 1870s and also with goodlooking spire.

GALGATE

Right by Ellel is Galgate, a very fine example of a mill village and complete with extensive cottages for the Georgian and Victorian workers, larger properties for foremen and managers, and with a magnificent mill still complete.

In recent times it has had many new houses of various types put up to cater for Lancaster and Preston workers, and for the staff of the university which is just up the road.   The canalside district is now

busy thanks to the resurgence of canal pleasurecraft and we used to pick up boats here.   Good pub right by it characterises the simple pleasures of canal cruising !   The old mill pond with its shading trees used to be a favourite spot for watching bats on long summer evenings.

CONDER GREEN

A hamlet of farms and cottages with one pub, the Stork, set in the remote coastal district east of the A6.   The student fraternity used to frequent the Stork provided they could cadge a lift on long spring or summer evenings, and many a jolly night used to be had there.   After a gap of 10 years I returned to lecture at the campus, and stayed the night at the Stork: we were the only people there on a lonely winter night, and very eerie it was too !

The diminutive Conder river is here tidal and goes into great mud and grass flats: there used to be a family living on a big, beached, boat down from the pub.

Endless horse riding and walking possibilities from here since it was easy to ride, given a low tide, across the Lune's expanses to the Overton district: nice in warm weather at least, when the horse would swim with you !

THURNHAM

The riding stables were by the bridge over the
canal branch down to Glasson in this dispersed and small
settlement of farms and cottages. The hall is one
of those interesting, remote, old places, basically
a 16th century edifice given a new facade in the
early 19th century and not much altered thereafter.

GLASSON

Pleasure craft and a few working boats use this
little port, a creation of the 1780s thanks to the
rich business families of Lancaster who saw it as their
way to beat the rapidly silting Lune estuary. Its
impact was enhanced by the 1820s branch canal, complete
with 6 or 7 locks, that links it several miles to the
Lancaster canal at Galgate and thence north to
Kendal and Lancaster or south to Preston and the
midland system.

Something of a time capsule round the basin
because the original properties survive so well,
Glasson is an interesting little village settlement.
We used to swim on this length of canal because it
seemed so clean, as does Glasson harbour itself.
It never gained great amounts of business, as one would
not   expect so remote a place to do so: no big town
or industries nearby.

SUNDERLAND

One of the remotest of remote coastal places
is the settlement of Sunderland - literally a land
asunder thanks to the vagaries of tide and weather
cutting it off. With landing problems up river at
Lancaster this was the point - using jetties ,
packhorses and the like- that cotton was first
landed to be taken up to Lancaster for processing in
the mills.

Various later 17th and 18th century
properties survive, but what a forsaken place it seems
to be ! The grave of the black slave Sambo (a freeman
here of course, as slavery did not exist in theory in
the country) is at Sunderland too, dating from the
18th century.

OVERTON

If Sunderland was too remote you could stop
at Overton, with various Georgian properties ranging
from farmhouse down to humblest cottage, and again
cut off by tide. I always used to wonder who could
live here permanently ! The church is remote from
the houses and is mainly a Norman survival and
an interesting one too.

Masses of open space for walking or riding
beckons from here to the Lune estuary, but you need
to have a guide since dangerous currents and quick
sands are all about.

QUERNMORE

Pronounced by the locals as Quormor, when we used to visit, the little settlement is best known for its hall - this is a classical style, nicely balanced, mansion of the 1790s with the standard picturesque grounds and views from the heights. It used to have various Anglican monks attached and they would attend courses at the university, bringing colour and creativity to the experiences of us youngsters since they were of unusual calling, guise, views and often from abroad !

BARE

Now surrounded by Morecambe's modern growth is the old village of Bare, still with a villagey feel, and with some 17th and 18th century cottages and houses to bear witness to its heritage belied by recent housing. At one edge you can still get straight into open fields and then on to Hest Bank along a pleasant bridle path.

TORRISHOLME

Another older place swamped by Morecambe and modern growth is Torrisholme. I stayed for 6 months in a bungalow here, walking the landlady's ancient dog up the little open field system that led onto rising land behind the road. The housing could be anywhere in Britain, with just odd older houses left behind in indiscriminate growth of the urban mass.

HALTON

Halton was once a village set by the lovely river Lune in rural district: the inexorable growth of Lancaster under the impact of the industrial revolution, and the usefulness of the river in powering and watering industrial concerns, led to the development of extensive industries along the Lune on both sides, and to the creation of Halton as   industrial and suburban neighbour to Lancaster.

Good riverside walks, but industry is all about in a limited way.

Nice Victorian parish church which has retained much inside from the old fabric now gone; fascinating churchyard mound, with evidence of Norman and Roman occupation here, famous Halton cross of the 11 th century, and so on.

The village displays much modern housing as well as industrial archaeological specimens, and a number of 17th, 18th and early 19th century houses that add much to the attractiveness of the place. Well worth looking round before going either into Lancaster or the open country nearby.

CATON

Favoured by many of the Lancaster professional
families is Caton, a village in the first reaches of the
Lune valley east of the city. Even in this rural retreat
there are mills and some industrial concerns, both old
and modern, but they are sheltered by the woods and
slopes, and do not detract from the many pretty
alleys, lanes and streets of the village.

Sadly the church is in fabric not very
interesting, though awash with furnishings from the old
church which must have been immeasurably more worth
looking round. The church is actually next door to
Caton in Brookhouse, another goodlooking village.
The river Artle adds to the charms of the place as it
winds down to the Lune, as do the walks and the parkland
setting .

One of the pleasantest houses is Gresgarth
Hall, to the south in woods above the Artle: a hall
of 18th and early 19th century vintage.

CLAUGHTON

Claughton has the distinction of its aerial
ropeways carrying dumpers up on to Claughton Moor and
its quarries - you can't miss them above the road.
It is set on the rising land above the Lune's flat
valley bottom, and there is further industrial
development there.

The village shows   interesting older
houses and cottages, a well known inn much used in

coaching times, and a parish church mainly of the 1700s.
According to all the books most of the hall was simply
removed to the top of a nearby hill this century !

WRAY

We were in this village a week ago walking
round and risking the cars which whizz   down narrow
road full of bends as if on the M6. It used to be
known as the most immoral place of the Lune valley with
a vast illegitimacy rate, according to local historians !
The village is a line of houses and cottages on both
sides and apparently of the 18th and early 19th centuries-
most appealling and today highly prized rural homes.

HORNBY

We have had many lunches over the years in this
village's pub, an inviting hostelry below the castle,
close to many desirable period houses in this Lunesdale
settlement. The river skirting closest by is the
Wenning just near to its confluence with the Lune, and
with the rising land, vistas and woods the whole place
is picturesque in the extreme.

In the village street the parish church is an
odd little building, consisting of east and west ends by

Edward Stanley - a rare polygonal apse and an octagonal
tower, and of c1514. They were built at his expense as
thanksgiving for his part in defeating the Scots at
Flodden in 1513. Several 19th century efforts added
the main church in between, but nothing jars.

Over the road is the little RC chapel,
with a big house for the priest attached, and each of
the early 19th century with quite showy Venetian windows
and substantial outbuildings.

The castle rises above the village out of
the trees, really looking quite splendid from any direction. The rear is an evident fortified c1300 pele
with alterations of the 16th century, whilst the facade
of the Victorian years is by Austin and Paley after
a country house fire had burned down most of the
earlier work by Paley and his senior partner Sharpe.
The most noticeable thing is the tower or turret
that hits you.

The village was home to the famous RC
priest John Lingard, author of history books on
the country and getting a memorial in the Anglican
parish church (he died in 1851) which must be some sort
of record. Lingard was an illustrious scholar and
priest in his day. It says much for the status and
standing of the RC faith that most of Lancashire was
fairly friendly towards it in past centuries, unlike
so many regions and counties.

WENNINGTON

An under-rated village of nice houses set
along the under-rated little river Wenning as it comes
from Bentham and Yorkshire just a mile or two away.

Rather like an estate village, Wennington has its big
house, in this case one of the Victorian years.

TUNSTALL

Known to me for its charming parish church,
on a slant to the winding main road, Tunstall is
a picturesque little village between the rivers Lune
and Greta not long before the county boundaries with
Westmorland and Yorkshire. The road detours in a wide
ark round the parkland setting for Thurland Castle,
which is very hard to see thanks to skilful planting of
woods and copses, and use of the lay of the land.

The castle is apparently early medieval,
rebuilt and fortified more in the 15th century, and then
attended to by the architect Sir Jeffrey Wyattville
in the early 19th century - a common fate for most
medieval structures was this beautifying !

The castle was burned out later that century
and Paley and Austin provided a suitably grand rebuild
of the 1870s and 1880s for the North family. And very
good too it looks.

The notorious school for girls founded by
William Carus Wilson, and attended by several Bronte
girls, was originally here - the buildings now being
cottages - and one wonders what the man's many
descendants thought at the portrayal of the school and
master in later years ! The exact position was by the
bridge at Cowan Bridge up the road from Tunstall, but
the owner and founder was incumbent of Tunstall, of
this parish which took in Cowan.

An odd episode: how true was it one wonders ?

WHITTINGTON

The fine parish church at this border parish is set on the steepest of sites looking down the valley and on the Westmorland boundary just out of Kirkby Lonsdale. Something of an estate village since it still has its model and modern estate housing and big house, Whittington is a pleasant place for a Sunday picnic in the sun - which we have had there several times in this year's fickle summer !

The road detours round the foot of the parkland setting for the hall of the late Georgian era but already in Tudor style. Model cottages all over the place, and round the side and back of the hall a nice steep road past the parish church and more handsome, well cared for, properties.

The local family, the Greens, paid for a Victorian rebuild of a late medieval fabric so far as the church is concerned: what interests me is the way that the Lune valley landowners have allowed very little access to the river according to the maps - miles and miles of high hedges and wire fences, walls and gates against trespassers and really quite discouraging ! Still, a historic village.

ARKHOLME

Continuing down the left, eastern, side of the Lune into Arkholme, you find a most fortunate village which has developed along a delightful village street away from the main road and down to the river Lune as far as the parish church - and with access to the river too ! A true bonus.

This is a particularly interesting spot on

the river because here it has several branches as the bed has moved and these other artieries siezed up. Thus it was that, with us in attendance, a keen and unwise geological student forded the river at what is one of the ancient fording points in the valley,more than 20 years ago !

We all made it - it being a dry summer - to live to tell the tale !   A lovely place.

The village has a display of 17th and 18th century houses of modest, even humble, proportions, plus a nice medieval church, and a proud hall of the 1840s - Storrs Hall.

OVER KELLETT

Yet another charming village is Over Kellett, a little too close to the M6 but awash with attractive village stone houses including a wide range from humble 3 or 4 roomed ones to quite large properties. The church is medieval but as is so often the case, greatly attended to in a "restoration" last century.

NETHER KELLETT

Rather too close to the M6 for comfort and with the motorway sweeping past its sloping eastern side is

this village close to the county boundary. It achieved
fame in that decade thanks to being the set for a well
known children's ghost-comedy series (THE GHOSTS OF
MOTLEY HALL, from memory) and in it the hall played the
chief role.

Snug little cottages peer from round inviting
backways to entrance the visitors (of which there are
not that many usually); the star is the hall, now in
county council usage, and rarely open to visitors.
I have twice been able to look round its pele tower
core, of the c1300 era, now encased in a fine 1590s
style Elizabethan coat. It is an excellent combination
of stone and timber to make one of those unmistakably
Lancastrian halls.

Stabling, gatehouse and outbuildings add to
the ensemble, built by the Bindloss family of
merchants. Inside, there is a haunted wing in which
few will sleep easily, reputedly used for housing the
line of deformed children of the family in earlier
centuries and who somehow lived to great ages locked
away in their cells !   Another person is supposed to be
buried inside the thickness of the stone centre of the
great staircase !

What a place for hauntings !

The canal winds disarmingly through the
village: go a short way to the south along it and you
come to one of those inviting arms of the waterway which
lead to the old quarries - but watch you go by rowing
boat since we got grounded there once.

Woods and wildlife abuund, and this stretch of
the canal was where , on warm, clear sunny days, you
could watch the shoals of fish swimming along - a very
rare thing indeed, but common up this end.

Lovely walks abound here.

CAPERNWRAY

More an estate than a village, Capernwray
has that beautifully designed aqueduct for the canal
as it wends its way over the steeply plunging little
river Keer. Quite delightful, as are the walks and the
woodland, the estate housing, farms, and the hall of
the 1840s and built by Sharpe of Lancaster (when he
was not playing at steamtrains etc ! he was a noted
architect).

PRIEST HUTTON

We would walk to this village each annual
canal holiday to enjoy the scenery - all very pastoral
still, and running upto the Westmorland border. Quite
large and stone built, the village enjoys good views
from its rising and falling site.

WARTON

A big village on the land rising upto the
famous Warton Crag, this one has been able to lose not
only the railway line but also the A6 and M6 well to its
east. The Crag, a very craggy cliff and hill, provides
a vantage point used by the hill fort people for their

prehistoric defences: the wooded slopes today provide a picturesque backdrop to a popular residential village just north of Canrforth.

The Crag used to mark the Lancashire boundary and the end of the M6 for years, and told Lancastrians they were either coming home or going abroad ! Lovely walks round it, and a web of narrow roads invitingly ring its lower slopes.

The village street is most satisfying in its architecture running from the 15th into the 19th centuries. At one end the parish church is generally medieval, but is embarrasingly upstaged by the rectory nearby : this is a 14th century pele of some quality, with medieval additions also. The facade makes it more modern and far more comfortable. The whole was a manor house type c1300.

The place is visited by Americans thanks to the Washington family links.

SILVERDALE

For 150 years genteel families have come to this coastal place for holidays: Mrs Gaskell, the Knutsford and Manchester novelist friend of Charles Dickens, often stayed here in the early Victorian years and many links with the district figure in her letters and books.

Several notable vantage points offer superb views over Morecambe Bay in different directions, and the sunsets are famous. Do not expect a seafront: instead

there are hundreds of acres of open marsh and sand for walking. Lots of new developments have not ruined the village feel: plenty of attractive older cottages and houses vie with Victorian and 20th century. A favoured place for retirement, this one.

YEALAND REDMAYNE

Yealand Redmayne does not offer the great house that is its neighbour's province, but it is attractive enough and benefits from sloping land, views and Crinklebarrow Woods behind.

YEALAND CONYERS

This village shows off some of the best villagescape of the county and is highly prized as a residential quarter. It too has escaped the impact of the main roads and railway and is surrounded by charming little roads and lanes that invite the inquisitive: sadly the parish church does not match up to the houses ! It is a plain 1830s effort, and is poor by comparison with the pleasant Quaker meeting house of the 1690s and typical of so many put up between Lancaster and Kendal districts.

If you can, walk up the steep gradient on the backlane between Conyers and Warton, for from that vantage point there is a magnificent panorama of Leighton Hall and its sweeping parkland setting. This is a noble house, built in mid 18th century Georgian, then given its present much admired look thanks to work of 1810 for the furniture maestro Richard Gillow.

Paley and Austin enlarged what was a pretty but modest hall into something much larger, but did it tastefully in the 1870s.

You remember the turrets and battlements, the pavilion wing, the graceful staircase and interior pillars, the woodwork and screens, the towers and cast ironwork. Utterly charming.

RAMPSIDE

ON the severe bend of the main coast route from Barrow in Furness to Ulverston is Rampside, with good views across Morecambe Bay and the peninsula of Foulney Island nearby. Some 17th and 18th century houses mingle with considerable 20th century growth as folk could find building plots !

BARDSEA

Bardsea has one of the finest situations for a church - superb views included - but an oddly unsatisfying design by one of the Kendal Websters (and thus 19th century). Some interesting historical connections link the place with Conishead priory up the road and the countryside is welcoming and rewarding if you explore on foot.

URSWICK

One of the ancient and important parishes of medieval Furness, Urswick's chief interest is its several prehistoric sites and above all the parish church: not only an impressive medieval stone fabric but awash with interior interest including outstanding work by C R Ashbee's Camden Guild of the 1900s (he being of Chipping Campden fames in the mould of Morris, Burne Jones et al).

A pleasing village centre too.

LINDAL IN FURNESS

Mining and quarrying village north of Barrow.

Rows of cottages and terraced houses, but with a village green oddly enough dating from the preindustrial days.

BLAWITH

Old rural and mining community set along the main road to Coniston in spectacular mountain scenery, Blawith is awash with traditional cottages and farms, often occupied by commuters or as second homes.

TORVER

A village split by the improved main route from Broughton to Coniston, and with one of thoe most interesting and rewarding of Victorian parish churches. The 19th century vicar for many years, called Ellwood, wrote extensively on the parish in several books and on other topics too (like Iceland and Norway and local history). He also left detailed accounts of life in this sort of fairly remote village in the mid and later 19th century. Essential reading !

SEATHWAITE

World renowned thanks to its portrayal in William Wordsworth's EXCURSION and other poems, Seathwaite remains typical of lakeland villages in its remote beauty and isolation for most of the year - except when surges of tourists clamber all over it in good weather !

Wonderful Walker was incumbent here for much of the 18th century and early 19th, and eking out a tiny lakeland stipend doing any job available and required. He was typical in his life and work of the many men serving poor lake district incumbencies for centuries.

The stone and slate houses and cottages have tended to become second or holiday homes and thus in the last 100 years the inheritance of the previous thousand has been lost.

The scenery is what you would expect of one of the most beautiful of valleys with the river Duddon passing down.

FAR AND NEAR SAWREY

Spectacularly beautiful is the setting for Far and Near Sawrey, the latter looking out to charming Esthwaite Water, the former closer to the ferry across Windermere, and world famous for their being the haunt of that illustrious lakeland author and landowner Beatrix Potter.

Hill Top farm at Near Sawrey is the big attraction
thanks to its occupation by Mrs Potter; but both villages
present, out of season, the type of backlanes and
lonnings that invite pedestrian exploration to admire
the plants, trees and shrubs which find the climate so
acceptable.   A wealth of flora and fauna, the things
that encouraged the authoress, plus all those quaint
farmhouses and cottages, and of course the lakes and
hills.

        Many big houses also grace the district,
mostly Edwardian and Victorian mansions. In the
district there is a great deal to see for the tourists:
a few years ago it was all relatively peaceful except
in high season, but not now !

RUSLAND

        IN the wild district between Coniston and
Windermere runs the Rusland Pool, a picturesque stretch
of lakeland water with some of the wildest habitat
and flora and fauna of the country   The village is
small and worth exploring on foot.

SATTERTHWAITE

        One of the settings (perhaps THE one) for
the hugely popular POSTMAN PAT series of books and
films, Satterthwaite is made up of grey stone cottages

and farms, and looks at its best when the autumn mists
and swirling smoke from fires fill the sky and
air.   Once this was a gunpowder making place , a place
of iron works, charcoalmaking and the like. Now it
is all tourists with a bit of farming and a lot of
forestry.

        It is surprising how remote it can be if
you escape the carbound tourist horde !

FINSTHWAITE

        In the same wooded district is Finsthwaite,
again a smattering of old cottages and farms and with
industrial archaeological remains from the various
woodland and other trades which once abounded here.
This is real SWALLOWS AND AMAZONS territory !

NEWBY BRIDGE

        One tourist trap is the narrow old bridge here
at the foot of Windermere, famous for its cleverly
sited old coaching inn the Swan, complete today with a
vast array of tourist goodies !   The inn is generally
18th, the bridge 17th, century. Plethora of new housing
and developments, but they do not spoil the old village
look. This was a busy industrial area into this century

for woodland trades like bobbin making, gunpowder and
bark crafts - and earlier on, ironmaking.

CARTMEL FELL

For my money this is the most glorious
district of the lakes, for not only are tourists
relatively few throughout the year, and those that do
get here are either carbound or lost, the scenery is
a star turn and the place has hardly any jarring
modern development. The church is an exquisite
woodland creation of a humble parish, built in the 1500s
in local vernacular style.

In the area are many hidden 16th, 17th and 18th
century properties, all hard to find but lovely;
and true big houses of modern vintage - like the pair
by the illustrious Voysey - are so discreet as to be
all but invisible.

Be warned: take a good map ! Cartmel Fell
is how most of the lake looked into the 19th century,
and the properties, here dispersed, became joined up
by incessant growth.

HAVERTHWAITE

Our 3 small children love this railway place at

the foot of Windermere. It is a small place and now
packed thanks to its lakeside railway line that links
remotest lakeland woods with the big Windermere
steamers. Next door is Backbarrow, equally a place of
former lakeland woodland trades, and in the 18th century
of some fame thanks to its being the place of work
of the illustrious Wilkinson ironworks. At Lindale
to the south the enormous iron monument to the family
is on show.

HIGH NEWTON

Ruthlessly affected by the driving of the
improved A590 through its middle, High Newton would
otherwise be a pretty stone and slate village on the
fells above Cartmel and Grange. It is also a place
favoured for second and holiday homes.

FIELD BROUGHTON

The church and parsonage of this dispersed
village are isolated, forming a handsome Victorian
pair in the pleasant countryside between Grange and
Windermere. Several big houses and scattered smaller
houses make up the village.

LINDALE

Climbing up the craggy hillside of awful
gradient is Lindale in Cartmel, with the new bypass
making it quieter, almost deserted at times. It is a
charming place for wandering down backalleys, and
we holidayed at one of the old mining cottages so
lovingly converted into modern house. Fabulous views,
excellent climbs, fine pubs and houses clinging to
the steepness, and a parish church whose main interest
lies in its links with the Websters of this area and
Kendal, amongst the best known of regional architects.

FLOOKBURGH

A considerable and ancient village where the
coastal road swings violently inland, leaving the older
parts of the settlement undisturbed by modern traffic.
Flookburgh shows off many 17th and 18th century stone
and cobble, slate and other cottages and small houses,
with workshops and outbuildings suggesting that here was
a selfcontained and selfsustaining community which
relied both on farming and on the wealth of the sea
on Morecambe Bay.

From the surrounding coast people still go
after flukes or flatfish, shrimps and sea fish and
shellfish, usually on tractors today. An exciting
business with men pitted against the swift tide.

Next door to the sheltered garden nursery
is the big and bold parish church, another of the

fine efforts of Pale and Austin. We went round it this
afternoon, and over the road to the cemetery to view the
war graves of menserving alongside my father in the
RAF crews that practised here, and which lost so many:
my father is always moved when he sees their names, those
of his pals, 50 years later.

ALLITHWAITE

On the winding and narrow coast road from
Grange is Allithwaite, a quiet huddle of old lakeland
properties with many new ones, several pubs, and up
a steep hill the gloriously situated, and big,
expanse of the 1860s parish church, vicarage and
school - proud, but lacking the sort of character
and excellence that came to characterise the work
of E G Paley of Lancaster when he took into
partnership H J Austin several years later.

Victorian properties all around, mainly
either small cottages or big country houses.
Nice playground by the school.

KENTS BANK

Out of Grange you turn off the main coast

road and down to the little settlement of Kents Bank,
originally just a few fishing folk and their homes,
odd farms, and then the railway came: station,
workers' homes, then homes for the affluent of
industrial Lancashire and others, and much modern
development . Still, it makes a change from the
extensive ribbon development out of Grange with
hardly a thing behind the houses - just spoiled views !
But oh dear ! the endless lines of modern bungalows !

ILLUSTRATIONS

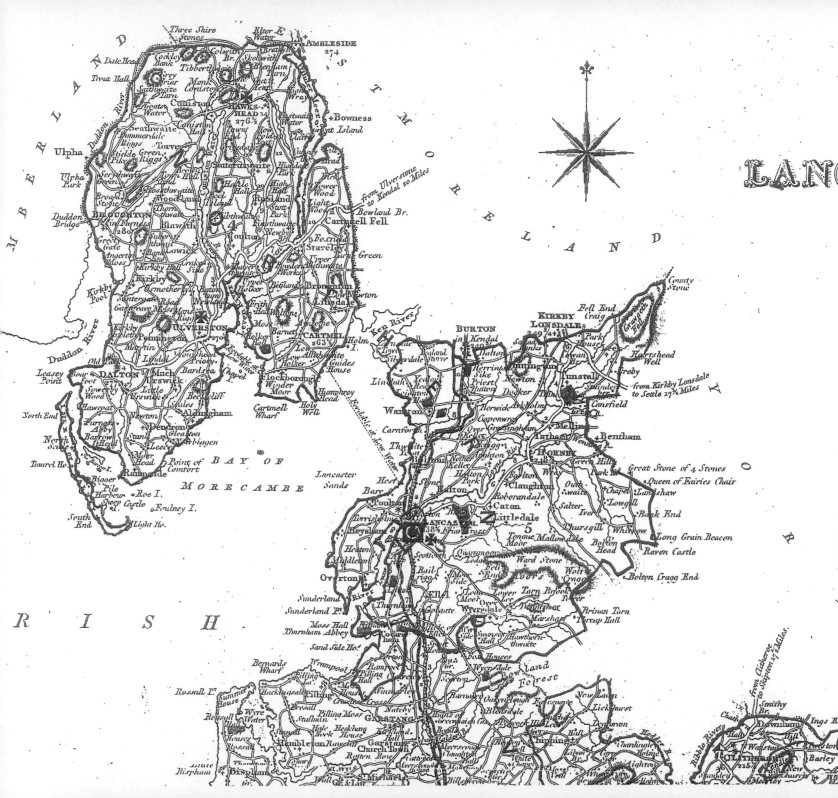

LANCASHIRE.

E A

RIVER RIBBLE

REFERENCE to the HUNDREDS.

Amounderness
Blackburn
Leyland
Lonsdale, N.th of the Sands
Lonsdale, S.th of the Sands
Salford
West Derby

POULTON 233¾

Blackpool

KIRKHAM 225½

PRESTON

BLACKBURN 209¾

HASLINGDEN 202¾

Great Harwood

BURNLEY 210

Wolf Stones

Brown Birks

from Colne to Bradford 28 Miles.

from Burnley to Halifax 21 Miles.

from Rochdale 16¼ Miles

from Halifax 16¼ M.

ROCHDALE 197

BURY

CHORLEY

WIGAN

BOLTON

SOUTHERN DIVISION

ORMSKIRK 209

Formby Point

South Port

Birkdale

LEIGH

OLDHAM

PRESCOT

LIVERPOOL 205

MANCHESTER

SALFORD

Rock Perch

Chat Moss

STRETFORD

River Mersey

STOCKPORT by Buxton 173¾ Leeds 178¼

London to by Bakewell Buxton Knutsford Leek

from Manchester to Halifax 25½ Miles

Lower Runcorn

RIVER D

C H E S H I R E

PART II

CONTENTS

        In the following pages I have presented my own choice of the historic towns of Lancashire, and have been eager to show off as many of the towns of my home county as possible in one book. It is indeed a rich inheritance, and much more could be written about the towns collectively and individually. I have spent most of my life living in the county or in ones next door to it, and have used these 40 years in studying the history : my visits to each town have been over a period of many years - readers, I know, will understand if their favourite bits and pieces are omitted ! Happy reading !

BURY

About 8 miles north of Manchester lies Bury
sandwiched between Bolton on the west and Rochdale on
the east. It was a substantial market town and
parish in the 1800s with a population in the town itself
of over 7,000 with 22,000 in the actual parish -
which covered four other townships as well as three
chapelries into Victorian times. Its principal work
was wool and the cloth trade in general until the
advent of cotton in the 18th century and the swift
takeover of mills by the new upstart and the many
inventions for it. The result was that Bury had in the
1820s 27 names listed as cotton manufacturers and
another 26 listed as cotton spinners in a variety of
parish locations.

At the same time there were 58 named firms of
woollen manufacturers: it would be interesting to find
out the scale of operations, numbers employed, size
of buildings and output of goods to determine which
was predominant, though writers had no doubts that
it was cotton. There were 19 firms which both
spun and weaved cotton, and the output was considerable.

It was Sir Robert Peel the elder who had founded
his cotton printing works on the banks of the river Irwell
and who was described as having enriched both himself,
his workers and the town of Bury in subsequent decades.
Cotton was held responsible for the rising population:
interestingly, a local census of 1773 recorded a total

Bury town population of 2,090, which meant that in 30
years the population had quintupled.

In the later 19th century and during the first
half of the present one Bury was a byword for cotton:
but it also had its engineering works, its dyeing
firms, bleaching premises, printing and woollen
manufactures, and its iron and steel foundries. One
could not say how many of these now survive for the
ferocious pace of economic change over the last 50
years has wreaked havoc with so many Lancashire towns
one-time dependent on staple industries. I do know
that Bury has a very human face, with human-scale
public buildings, plenty of good shoping districts
and centres, and modern attempts to present the worst
excesses of the past in a meaningful guise in their
museum and exhibitions. In any town it helps to have
a good site provided by nature, and this is the
case with Bury: townscaping and landscaping benefit
considerably form the slopes available !
So much that remains is Victorian as one would expect
in an industrial town, but the whole adds up to
the creation of a town centre worth the time and trouble
to visit - and the same can not be said of all of our
historic towns ! And the flowers and parks soften
the town too.

ORMSKIRK

The capital for a large tract of agricultural
Lancashire rich with vegetables and crops grown in
dark peaty soil, Ormskirk used to mark our halfway
to Southport from St Helens along one of the best and
quietist of main roads in the 1950s and 1960s. My
uncle and his family live not far from the road, and
in my childhood we used to call to see the grown up
charges who had been in my mother's care in the
town during the war. Their house was one of those
big ones with huge garden packed with childhood
delights like several ponds stocked with fish of all
varieties.

The town is an old marketcentre, and this
function continues to thrive alongside the old main
roads which meet at the little clocktower - in my
youth the market was a great attraction and used to
impede the traffic something terrible. By the 1820s
it is listed as having several cotton firms, furniture
businesses, hat makers, roperies, and above all
pubs and inns. It has listed all the many economic
activities one would expect of such a centre. The
saddest thing about the place is that so little that is old
has been preserved.

The parish church hits one from the main
road, since it possesses both spire and separate
tower. It is medieval - 13th to 15th century in the main -
with total restoration by Paley and Austin in the
1870s and 1880s. The Derby chapel contains the
vault for the medieval family bodies, the family then
living at now demolished Lathom hall out of town.
Most of the town appears to be Victorian or modern,
with not a lot to detain the historian even after a
long walk down back lanes and alleys - it was
ever the case I'm afraid, that the old was consigned to
rubble. This is even more strange when one thinks of
the modern prosperity of the place.

Outside the town lies the Edghill College,
vast brick buildings with metal windows and in my day
famous for having three times the usual number of
female students as against the men ! Not too far away
too is the famous water tower, which every traveller
knows. The neighbouring countryside, all in the
1820s under Ormskirk parish, possesses some rather
interesting pieces of architecture.

Latham used to be a frequent port of call
at festival time: Easter or Harvest or similar would
bring us to view the chapel, a very fine little
1500s building bedecked with flowers and displays of
woodwork and rarely visited by outsiders. On the rising
land in the distance remained the great service wing of
Lathom Hall, which was brought into the Stanley family
in the 1400s by marriage. The big rambling medieval house
remained the Stanley (earls of Derby) home into the
1640s when it received major damage at the hands of
the parliamentary forces and withstood a long siege.
It was evidently repaired to some extent, but was
abandoned by the Stanleys c1714 and came through several
hands before stopping with the Wilbrahams. They
rebuilt all in grand manner in the 1720s. The main rooms
were built in the grand style: hall 40 foot square by
30 high, library 50 by 21 feet, 13 bedroom apartments,
saloon 40 by 24. All was Paladian and Ionic classical
work to provide a central block of 13 bays and two
great service wings.

Now only one wing remains: sad really isn't
it ? Still the chapel is lovely , as are the nearby
almshouses. The garish flatroofed and mostly glass
research laboratories nearby are startling.

At Burscough was a small Augustinian priory
founded in the late 12th century , but whenever
I visited it, it really was a site that provided hardly
anything at all for the imagination:no ruins really.
The several 19th century parish churches established out
of Ormskirk are not too interesting either: but
there is Scarisbrick hall, one of the major achievements
of the age.

Scarisbrick hall in the 18th century was
a 16th century timber manor house owned by the
family of that name who were RCs. The hall was
added to and encased in stone c1815, then entirely
rebuilt from 1836 thanks to the designs of the young
architect A W Pugin. The result was one of those
fabulous Gothic masterpieces : great hall, towers
with finials, double bays on two floors, the sort of
fancies in windows and glass to be seen   in the
vastly larger houses of parliament; plaster, woodwork
and internal ornament of a richness that is stunning.
Substantial parts of the old house were left in tact
but the rebuilding created a spectacular new house
from most angles, and above all internally.

Sadly of course, perhaps inevitably, the
Scarisbricks sold up and this century most of the
interior was sold off in notorious asset stripping
during the 1960s. The case made headlines in local
papers.

Skelmersdale was the most distant township,
5 miles and more from Ormskirk and now an enormous
new town mainly for merseysiders. The district
was devastated by new roads too, and I recall many of
the old buildings either being knocked down or
stuck in the middle of unsuitable sights and sites.

WIGAN

Wigan was the great rival to St Helens in
rugby and all else, though the two are quite similar in
their industrial inheritance if not in age.   Wigan
is an ancient borough and thanks to coal , iron, steel,
other metal trades and cotton mills the place had
reached the considerable population of 11,000 in 1801
and 18,000 in 1821 - though its parish, which included
Billinge, Hindley, Pemberton and Upholland, had a
population of 25,000 and 38,000 at those respective
dates.

Architecturally there are some interesting and
outstanding parts of the town, though in my youth
during the 1950s and 1960s our regular trips for shopping
and site seeing revealed endless rows of blackened
terraced houses and public buildings. Things have
become better in this respect and a good deal more
attention given to the appearance of places.

The parish church is one of those big medieval
structures one would expect in an important ancient borough.
It is 13th century and later but much rebuilt in the
Victorian years when money was plentiful and taste
in short supply. The surrounding town centre streets and
alleys offer interesting walks, and down one was that
notable pet shop which displayed any number of exotic
birds and mammals which we could not afford.

We used to love the old market hall, now part of the enormous rebuilding of the centre - just look at the Galleries shopping centre - and new civic life. Wigan Pier is now a star - really a sort of loading siding on the canal - and with its renovated wharves and warehouses in busy use by locals and offcomers. Museums and exhibitions are a big thing now in the town - the showpiece centres on the Pier district with its steam engines, boats, museum, shops and such things as actors showing how it all was ! The good old days ! Just look too at the chapels and churches of other denominations - in such a large parish most newcomers could find a church to their liking - several Methodist connexions, Congregational and Presbyterian, Baptist and others.

Wigan was HQ for county royalists led by the earl of Derby in the 1640s and 1650s, and was scene of one of the last skirmishes of the civil wars. 70 years later it was one of the Jacobite centres in the county and in the '15 it had a clutch of hangings for the locals to witness. It was left untouched by the new rebel Jacobite army in 1745, though they did march through it on their way to Derby.

At a more mundane level, Wigan had a proper waterworks from 1761 thanks to a local private works, a wide variety of schools - industry, dame, grammar, free and so on - a fine library, gasworks, mechanics institute and all the trappings that one would expect in a prosperous (if mucky) Georgian market borough. Within the parish but beyond the town were some places of particular interest.

Haigh hall is the foremost, and made much of nowadays. The hall was the property of the Bradshaighs from the 13th to 18th centuries, when about 1770, with the end of the line, the lot went to the wealthy earl of Crawford and Balcarres (of Culzean fame and fortune in Ayrshire). The new owner enjoyed vast income from his coal mines both here and in Ayrshire; his succesor, the 24th earl, rebuilt the hall in the 1830s and 1840s, creating a monumental hall more or less 11 bays square and magnificently sited in hundreds of acres of parkland. Today it is a tourist trap with golf course, endless walks, animals, flowers and so on. I recall the fishpond as having the most fabulous golden orfe one could

imagine, and they always rose to take bread with a swish and swirl like small sharks. The hall has long been used for receptions - lucky married couples ! - and the like.

The extensive parish included the heights of Ashurst Beacon, one of those fine beacons put up to send signals if the country were invaded. As a youngster I delighted in racing to the top of the hill followed by our dogs, and the beacon was simply a small pinnacled stone lump in rotten repair - but the views were stunning. Nowadays in better repair and with rather more housing, it is especially good for walking. On the next ridge is Parbold, and views to Wigan and other towns from each, and to the little (and then heavily polluted) river Douglas. It is the skylarks roundabout I remember best. It was also the area that the richer folk of the district wished to live in !

Billinge too, on the St Helens boundary, offered its "lump" or beacon, with woods and abandoned quarries nearby - a real adventure playground, though enormous new estates have encroached hereabouts. Abram is utterly urban; Winstanley, Orrell and other of the townships retain some fields amidst the sea of housing partly because mining subsidence makes the fields unsafe for building. Upholland is another urban area, with a bit of history as a small Benedictine priory in the middle ages .

WIDNES

Widnes is new: everything about was more or less commenced in the mid and late Victorian years, and especially this century: houses and public buildings, churches and industrial premises, parks and pleasant corners. It remains the sheer scale of the chemical industry and its effects which both impresses and appalls.

In the early 19th century Widnes was simply a township of the enormous parish of Prescot, and without even a chapel of ease. The population, with Appleton, was about 1,000 in 1801 and 1,500 20 years later. What happened to Widnes was its growth into a considerable chemical town with all the consequent drawbacks which this entailed.

One only has to look at what was happening round Northwich with Brunner Monde to appreciate the devastation and employment brought to this district of north Cheshire and southernmost Lancashire: many parts of them remain poisoned, especially the rivers. The main route into Cheshire and Wales used to be via Widnes, which also has the rail link from Merseyside to London. Views were and are everywhere: of the great Mersey river and ship canal, acres of sand and mud and water at any time of day, vistas down to Warrington and other towns, but above all the chemical industry of the town.

Today things are improved, but the spillages of dangerous chemicals continue to bedevil the cleansing of the town; new roads have ruined what there was of the way in attractive streets; and it figures near the bottom of tourism's places to visit. One redeeming feature is the museum of the chemical industry, another is the fine road bridge which replaced the old transporter.

WARRINGTON

Warrington, now forever sundered from its true county, used to stand on the border with Cheshire right on the Mersey. Unlike several of its neighbours (Widnes and St Helens for example) it was a considerable town at the time of the first census in 1801 with nearly 11,000 inhabitants, and the figure had risen to nearer 14,000 20 years later. It was a Roman centre, and for centuries was the chief fording point for miles of the considerable river Mersey. The first earl of Derby paid for the 15th century bridge, which was replaced in the 18th, 19th and 20 th centuries by successive structures to link the two counties. This bridge and the town which protected it, were seen as twin keys to control of Lancashire in the Civil Wars of the 1640s and 1650s, and during the two main Jacobite rebellions in 1715 and 1745.

Though considerable numbers of older properties have gone thanks to 19th and 20th century development, the town does have some left. It has also had all the trappings of an important town (like Wigan): libraries and grammar schools in the 17th and 18th centuries, Unitarian (a real sign of advanced learned society !) Congregational, several Methodist, Baptist, Quaker and RC chapels in the 1820s, plus an aristocratic Countess of Huntingdon's Connexion place of worship; and the figure of

2500 pupils at Sunday schools in the 1820s, which suggests the usual vastly youthful population of industrial Lancashire.

The famous Warrington Academy for Protestant Dissenters (principally Presbyterian, Congregational and the like) was established here in the 1670s and in new purpose built premises in the 1760s; it was the sort of place which everyone wanted to attend whatever their religious faiths since the quality of teaching was far higher than anywhere else.

There were other signs too of a flourishing provincial centre c1820: gas works, scientific and literary society, all sorts of relief agencies for the poor and needy, savings and other banks, market and town hall, cloth halls, assembly rooms and theatre, any number of religious agencies and missionary bodies. The old method of improving a town - lighting, paving, policing, getting rid of nuisances and the like - was by having a private Improvement Act passed (after 1835 an elected council in boroughs did the work): this happened thanks to Warrington's civic leaders in 1813.

The town's employment was based on its many market functions plus the textile trade. It had been coarse linen in the 17th century, but this had been abandoned for best linen, then progressively for sail cloth (the river offered openings though the town was not a port), and into cotton and cotton products like velveteen and muslins. Warrington was long a tanning industry (for leather), as well as possessing the famous Greenalls brewery and glas making. Malting, pin making, sugar refining and copper works had also been main employers at various times.

Directory lists show the plethora of trades and occupations in the 19th century town.

Architecturally there is more to see than in many of the South Lancs towns. Several squares of later Georgian buildings, individual houses and premises and churches, and above all the town hall in its fine floriforous setting.

The present town hall was one of James Gibbs'
designs in best classical tradition, a job done in
best quality bricks, with a giant central portico to
the roof ridge, and with the finest of iron railings and
gates: it is by far the premier building of the borough.
J W Patten, lord Winmarleigh, was MP for south Lancashire
for much of the early Victorian period, and this was
his home before retirement to Winmarleigh up in the north
of the county (and now an agricultural college). It
was he who is credited with agreeing to be a Tory
Irish secretary of state provided he did not have to
go there (he detested the country), and who stated that
it really was never in anyone's interest to engage in
expensive political contests: all should be decided upon
by the gentlemen before a contest was needed ! He liked
a quiet life, was extremely moderate in his views,
and very popular ! The hall came to the town in the
1870s and looks magnificent.

My impressions of the place ? I have never
been through the centre without that vast overweening
pong of beer and hops !   ah ! memories.

ROCHDALE

Rochdale was one of the largest of Lancashire
parishes and in 1801 had a population of 29,000
people, increased to 47,000 in 1821 thanks to the
booming cotton and woollen trades of the district.
The parish comprised 9 townships and 3 chapelries,
and is old enough to have figured in the Domesday survey
of the 1080s. As one would expect in a town of so many
people and townships, there was a very active municipal
life and the market town in the 1820s had all those
institutions that would be expected in any successful
provincial town: theatre and billiard rooms, newsroom
and library, assembly rooms, savings bank and
others, grammar and other schools, and a number of
charitable and voluntary benefit societies for the poor,
needy, sick and elderly.

It also had (and has) many churches: not only
Anglican but several shades of Methodists, Congregationalists,
Quakers, Unitarians, Roman Catholics, Baptists and
Countess of Huntingdon's amongst others: and towards
4,000 pupils were in the denominational Sunday schools
of the day.

The town retains a number of old buildings which
are well preserved. St Chad's parish church ranks amongst
the best, and stands on Sparrow Hill overlooking the
town centre. It is a fine church though its medieval
appearance is thanks to extensive rebuilding in the 19th

century to recreate the sort of 15th century wool church style of loftiness with airiness and statelisness. Quality stonework, big east window, west tower, plenty of stained glass, solid buttresses, and a history of disputes between the vicars and the local Dissenters over church rates and tithes : it figures prominently in any work on those two contentious topics. I should add that next door and now within the town is Middleton, which too has a good parish church - St Leonard's, again the subject of much restoration work to a medieval fabric and with a peculiar stumpy tower of wood and stone.

Of the many public buildings the town hall takes pride of place for it is one of the biggest, most impressive and most expensive of the type outside the giant cities. It was decided by the energetic and forward looking town council to have a new town hall in 1864, and as in the usual way, a competition was held to see which was the best design available. Crossland of Leeds won it, but the £20,000 which had been apportioned to cover the total outlay was found to be pitifully inadequate.

The result was that it cost a vast £155,000: but for that the town got a building of great splendour, with 240 foot spire, a mass of stone and marble of the best quality, and a main front over 300 feet long. It was opened in 1871, but a fire in the 1880s necessitated a replacement tower by Alfred Waterhouse - funds would only run to 190 feet of it, so 50 feet were lost.

The police court, the wool exchange and other offices were originally placed within the town hall, and its interior is if anything far grander than the exterior: well worth a guided trip round. An interesting lesson in overspending too !

One just has to associate Rochdale with the cooperative stores pioneers in their Toad Lane store: every Lancashire schoolchild used to learn about their efforts in 1844 to avoid the gross adulterations of food and drink and the excessive prices of the truck system with their selfhelp shop. The old shop and its adjacent buildings have been converted into a

museum and meeting rooms. In fact many of the smaller buildings of the centre have enjoyed something of this sort of renaissance in the last 10 or 15 years, in the credit of their town and owners. And the creative rejuvenation of unpromising buildings includes the splendid firebrigade museum housed when I saw it inside the actual present firestation: well done !

The directories list the array of talent and activity in the town: serried ranks of attornies, academies, boot and shoe makers, butchers and bakers, millers, dyers, flannel manufacturers by the score (150 in the 1820s), 100 and more pubs and inns of varying degree, woolstaplers and carders, cotton mill manufacturers and others. All impresses, and the town was arguably at its height in the 1820s and 1830s from the point of view of prosperity and advance. Certainly the manufacturers were prominent in local affairs, as writers noted.

There is only space to mention in passing such pleasures as the old Boar's Head inn at Middleton, which has 12th century origins and is now owned by the town council; Ninian Comper's 1900s work in the 1740s St Mary's church at Wardleworth; the art gallery on the Esplanade; relics such as the famous Blackstone Edge Roman road stretch on the moors; and the massive Ellenroad Ring mill, devoted to cotton spinning, and now restored to what it looked like in 1920.

BURNLEY

Burnley is one of the major towns of the county,
a medieval wool centre just by the Pennine range and
the river Calder valley; in the 18th century the cotton
industry arrived, and by the 1820s had supplanted the
traditional woollen trades as principal employer.
The population was under 3,500 in 1801 but towards 6,500
in the 1820s and over 80,000 in the 1940s.

Architecturally speaking the town displays
some good buildings as well as enormous Victorian and
modern rebuildings and redevelopments. St Peter's
church is basically medieval but with considerable work
from periods of restoration c1790, 1803 and the 1850s
which created a most pleasant and usable interior.
Plenty of 19th and 20th century churches for many
denominations show the destination of funds in those
days: the star of the district must be Townley hall,
a big medieval manor house with later additions
and alterations.

Townley (or Towneley) is of the characteristic
stone of the district, lines of battlements, big square
towers and porch in a heady mixture of medieval hall
generally altered thanks to fashion and whim in the early
17th century, the 1720s, and the 1810s. The display
is superficially Georgian, Jacobean and early Victorian
but the interior is now a museum and displays Elizabethan
long gallery, Regency drawing room and Jacobean rooms:
something for lovers of most important periods of decor !
The grounds, as with all the parks of the town, are
lovely.

A rival attraction, out of town near
Padiham, is Gawthorpe hall, built by the Shuttleworths
in the 1600s and looking like a giant square stone manor.
Nothing in the way of concession to later taste -
especially not Georgian - until the 1850s when Sir
Charles Barry did a drastic job of Gothicising it
all - parapet, heightening, much interior alterations.
The place is still notable, and again is put to new
use as conference and tourist and craft centre.

The town also boasts Burnley Mechanics Arts
centre, which is a brilliant conversion of the old
Mechanics Institute into a modern centre: then there
is the almost reborn section of the big Leeds Liverpool
canal, much revitalised in recent years for leisure.
The great cotton weaving mill in Queen Street is now
also a museum, but a working showpiece too, showing
how things were in the 1890s when cotton was flourishing.

The Weavers triangle is the renovated and
restored canalside district complete with spinning
mills and weaving sheds, foundries and warehouses,
workers' cottages, school and canal museum. A most
creditable exercise in industrial heritage, but it
(along with others) seemed to have very restricted
opening times.

BOLTON

Bolton is one of the major 3 or 4 urban areas of Lancashire and boasts a population in the borough of over 260,000. As at present constituted Bolton borough includes South Turton, Blackrod, Farnworth, Little Lever, Westhoughton, Horwich and Kearsley. The population of the two main pre-Victorian townships of Great and Little Bolton was also considerable in a county known for its big towns: 5,000 c1770, nearly 12,000 in the 1780s, 17,000 at the time of the first, 1801 census, 31,000 in 1821. The extensive parish as composed in the 1820s embraced 12 townships and 6 chapelries, and had long enjoyed the fruits, benefits, labour and profit of the industrial revolution.

For a start coal had been mined and used locally since the middle ages, and Flemish and other weavers had introduced the textile trades in the 14th century. Coal was abundant, as was building stone, water power, workers and customers. Manchester was 11 miles down the road with its network of roads, canals and later railways. The town's 17th century importance was well known and resulted in repeated fighting round it including the famous siege which resulted in the parliamentarian civilians being massacred by Royalist troops led by the wild Prince Rupert. A few years later, at the end of the second civil war in 1651, the royalist leader the earl of Derby was beheaded in the town for his part in war affairs.

I have often seen Bolton portrayed, sometimes anonymously, on film or TV. In my formative youth there were the two films SPRING AND PORT WINE, and THE FAMILY WAY in the late 1960s: the stories and acting apart, it was the sweeping landscape and townscape pictures of the town and its distant vistas of chimneys, terraced housing and above all the moors which impressed. And the accents of the stars were good too !

The mills of Bolton are famous. They included what is regarded as the last major mill to be built in the country, that of Sir John Holden's at Astley Bridge in the 1920s - what an error ! At the other extreme the town's oldest surviving mill seems to be that in Pool Street, which includes masonry and work of the 1770s in the St Helena Mill (presumably named in honour of Napoleon's last resting place !) It was thanks to the invention of a Bolton man, Samuel Crompton, that the Spinning Mule (a brilliant cross between two earlier machines, using the best ideas of each) created such a revolution in cotton spinning after 1779 - though in typical fashion Crompton made hardly a thing out of it all.

Bolton also claims to have had the highest factory chimney in the world: that of Blinkhorn's in Kay Street, put up in the 1840s and coming in at 367 feet. The Bolton leaflets inform me that it was used as the vantage point for Rothwell the painter to depict the town's superb setting. Bolton figures in union annals too, for the mill workers were amongst the first to form unions (though never called that name into the 19th century) to protect themselves. Thanks to industrial problems of the day the town had its share of troubles: about 1812 the Luddite riots when hundreds of men (led by the mythical Ned Ludd !) roamed the industrial districts causing damage to machinery which, it was believed, was putting so many out of work. People were hanged at Lancaster for damage to Bolton area property.

As popular politics continued to hold the stage for the 1830s and 1840s with a succession of movements, Bolton endured troubles with the Chartists in those decades, including a riot when the authorities refused to clamp down hard on the protesters (memories of Peterloo and Manchester in 1819 I should imagine terrified the mayor, and he may well have sympathised anyway with the protesters).

Bolton is proud of its past and shows it off to good effect. The local history museum is housed in what was the old town hall for Little Bolton, before the two (Little and Great) were united into one in 1838. National themes with local emphasis and examples here; the principal town museum also houses the art gallery and an aquarium (from memory) and covers a far broader spectrum of history including international ones. Bolton steam museum is housed in the Atlas Mills where their working machinery on show includes engines of 1840, 1860 and 1893 - steam engine enthusiasts will drool doubtless at the items !

The two stars must be Smithills hall and Hall i'th' Wood. The latter is a late medieval merchant's house, typical black and white timber framed, and of course known to all locally as the home of Samuel Crompton who invented the spinning mule in 1779. It has inside several rooms recreating particular aspects and periods of life - kitchen included. The hall possesses startlingly good displays of wooden panelling, household furniture, and concentrates on the 17th and 18th centuries. It seems too clean and uncluttered though ! Smithills is near an hotel which we used to visit for excellent meals; the after luncheon stroll was to the hall and round its grounds, which I recall as being free of fees for entry.

Smithills hall is a true manor house, with great hall of the 14th century, superb arrangements of Stuart and Elizabethan panelling and furniture, all formerly the Radcliffe household. A real jewel of the county's heritage.

Bolton town hall is one of those grand monumental edifices commenced in the 1860s and completed in the 1870s, when the Prince of Wales opened the place to great acclaim. The main parish church of St Peter is, sadly, wholly a building of the 1870s when Peter Ormrod of Bolton paid the gigantic amount of £45,000 for its construction. Imposing, but all the history has gone with the old one. I have not seen it, but hear that the Albert hall part of the town hall is being rebuilt in the best architectural traditions to replace the one destroyed in fire about 10 years ago.

Bolton has produced many characters of more than county fame, and one who needs mention is William Hesketh Lever, later Lord Leverhulme, who was born in Bolton in 1851 and worked in the family grocery business for a time. He went on to make an enormous fortune in soap and other chemical concerns, was ennobled, and did so much for this town as others where his factories were. Hence the bills for restoring Hall i' th' Wood, building schools and churches and houses and the like were all down to Lever. In our many journeys out north of home we used to see Rivington Pike beckoning in the distance: Leverhulme bought the Rivington hall and estate in 1904 and spent lavishly on what was meant to be for the people of Bolton, down below in the distance (though in fact Liverpool claimed it). If you have a chance, it is well worth a trip to see Lever's gardens and buildings.

Such a large town has much more to it than a few pages can suggest: any directory will tell the story of the plethora of activities going on at a particular date or in one epoch, for this was always a lively and progressive place

PRESTON

Preston first appears in my experience thanks to
seemingly endless traffic jams in the 1950s and early 1960s
as the A6, choking and clogging each town it traversed,
meandered via the town centre. It was the M6 which
liberated this and other towns of all sizes but I must
say that I missed the town centre on later visits due
to never coming within miles of it on the motorway:
all one sees are distant vistas of odd buildings or mills.

Preston is ancient: it was a Roman town and
throughout the middle ages of considerable importance
in the county. In between was a documented Anglo-
Saxon history including early churches and the like.
Preston was the main Fylde and district town at the
time of Domesday in the 1080s, and its 18th century
parish still covered Barton, Broughton, Grimsargh and
Ribbleton. What removed more or less the entire
signs of history earlier than 1850 was the onset of
industrialisation in the late 18th century and the
all-powerful destructive rebuilding by the Victorians.
The result is that there is scarcely anything in the
way of old buildings or historic remains, but just an
impression of money from the exceptionally large
20th century rebuilding and redevelopment schemes which
themselves often took away the Victorian remnants.
Above all into this century Preston was a cotton town,
benefiting from its sitting on the main road north and south.

Population of Preston was about 6,000 in 1780;
up to 12,000 in 1801, but acclerating thereafter to
25,000 in 1821. By 1851 it was 69,000 and well over
100,000 in the 1960s. Thereafter it was designated a
new town and grew considerably in both population
and acreage.

Architecturally Preston offers a few fine
streets and individual buildings. There are several
big and attractive parish churches of the mid Victorian
years, plus many Nonconformist and Roman Catholic
Victorian chapels. The corn exchange was the most
considerable public building when it was put up in
the 1820s but 60 odd years later it was the library
and museum put up in memory of E R Harris at a cost of
£80,000 which became the chief attraction. Harris
left his fortune to the town for cultural and charitable
purposes, and much of it went on this vast Classical
edifice.

The principal area of interest centres on
Winckley Square with the streets around it, and the whole
form what is regarded as a vital survivor of old Preston.
Most of the centre has not escaped massive redevelopment
in the 1960s and 1970s to create oceans of shops and
offices. The Georgian and later quarter which survives
is infinitely preferable from any point of view !

And finally for architecture there are a couple
of buildings not to miss. One is J A Hansom's
St Walburge of the 1850s. It has an enormous spire and
tower of 300 feet over the entrance porch more or less
in the middle of one side. Inside it is designed as
a hall for lectures rather than a church in the strict
meaning of the word. Quite an eyecatcher in and out !
The interior shows off an enormous hammerbeam roof,
all on view to the roof.

Then there is the equally remarkable St
Augustine's, an RC church, which displays a large
portico and pediment, and was embellished further
(50 years after its creation c1840) with twin towers on
either side of the portico and each topped with a
cupola. Another remarkable design using classical
motifs to effect.

So sudden and vast were the changes in 19th century Preston that the past was swept away. The cotton mills proliferated by the dozen: the first mill was introduced in Friargate in 1777 by Collison and Watson, but the industry took its major step forward with the firm of John Horrocks in 1791. Within a decade he not only had 6 big mills but had become MP for the borough and stood alongside Lord Derby's son Lord Stanley. This was the seemingly impossible leap socially which the manufacturing interest had taken in a few years. In those days opposition to such men in trade rising out of their position in society to rub shoulders with the county's finest was enormous: Horrocks did it, as others did after him, but he died young in 1804.

The Horrocks family firm were employing 4,000 workers by the 1820s, when the town had 40 cotton factories and mills mainly spinning cotton yarn. By the 1860s there were 77 such establishments split between weaving and spinning cotton about evenly. Today of course there is worry that any of the mills will survive since so many have already been lost.

Preston was always prominent in county affairs of national interest: Wars of the Roses, the Civil Wars of the 1640s and 1650s, the Jacobite rebellions of 1715 and 1745 and at other times. It is well known for its Preston Guild which meets only every 20 years - hence the saying, every Preston Guild. It was the home of the first teetotal movement amongst Preston's people concerned over the enormous social problems of drink - and the movement spread like wildfire thereafter from the 1820s. And it was one of the largest of parliamentary boroughs before the great Reform act of 1832, for the franchise was widespread and created a sort of democratic spirit. It was most unusual for this to be the case: the traditional franchise was open to all males over 21 who were not paupers and who had lived there for 6 months. The ensuing political battles (from the 1660s) require a book in themselves.

Preston to an extent lost its county flavour - that is its large number of gentry and county landed families who came to it on business, for entertainment and kept a town house there - once the cotton mills brought a coarseness and roughness associated with mill workers in every generation of urban Lancashire. The directories note this change: but it did not prevent the rise of Preston to importance as an industrial centre, nor did it prevent the rapid development of the railways of the district and eventually of the port facilities using the great Ribble estuary. I know what the writers meant: Lancaster even now seems far more refined, just that bit above the town in class ! I'm certain a few thousand Prestonians would disagree !

BLACKBURN

Blackburn might seem an unlikely tourist
town, but so it has proved to be over the last 10 years
and visitors come in numbers to examine its charms.
There is no getting away from its industrial past:
it has over 100,000 population - not that much growth
this century when one considers it had 63,000 in
1861, and 22,000 in 1821. It was a main cotton
town, and despite reliance on wool and similar items
in the middle ages, Blackburn and cotton became synonymous
in the later 18th and 19th centuries.

The parish in pre-Victorian decades comprised
not only Blackburn but 15 townships and 8 chapelries
with a vast population - 33,000 in 1801, by 1821
53,000. By the latter date it had the parish church
plus 10 Dissenting places of worship, plus all the
institutions and civic advances to be expected of a
market town which was already well known in the 16th
century: grammar school, Dissenting academy, theatre,
cloth hall and any number of charitable and religious
bodies.

Architecturally there is plenty to see.
The big old medieval parish church was, unfortunately,
demolished about 1820 and a new one built which would
accommodate more worshippers; this church in turn became
the nave of the cathedral church created in 1926,
and inside the sanctuary is now at the crossing of transepts
and nave.

The cathedral's great corona and other parts
are a product of the 1960s; there is a collection of
treasures, some of them on display, and the cathedral
diocesan offices are in the schools nearby.

The town continues to boast various other
churches: Roman Catholic, Nonconformist and Anglican
ones which include St John's of the 1780s. I once read
that the town hall had been described as "big,
Italianate and indifferent" ! It is rather more than
that, and for the 1850s very showy indeed.   Round
St John's is a conservation area which includes what
are left of the Georgian buildings in streets such as
Richmond Terrace and Victoria Street.   The principal
public hall is the King George's hall of 1913 which
seats around 2,000 and is venue for all sorts of
concerts and meetings.

The main museum and art gallery is well known
for its collections of Far Eastern material, strangely
enough, as well as its considerable local holdings.
Attention too is paid to the heritage of the Asian community in the district.   The smaller Lewis textile
museum in Exchange Street houses machines and replicas
showing the inventions of the industrial revolution.
Local artists too are catered for with a first floor
art gallery.

Just outside the town is Turton Tower, a very
impressive pele tower of the 15th century which
was integrated with previously freestanding buildings
of the time, in the 1590s, to create an Elizabethan
house.   The whole ensemble is most attractive black
and white timber framing with the big stone tower
attached. Inside it is every bit as pleasant: furniture
and furnishings of the period plus weapons and local
history material for the many tourists.   Far larger
and altogether in a different class is Hoghton Tower,
from the 1300s the Hoghton home.

Hoghton appears to be a mansion of the
16th to 17th centuries, surrounding two courtyards.
Apparently much work was done for the visit of James Ist
in 1617, when he and his hundreds of followers ate the
place out of all supplies and left problems for the owners

in the shape of refuse !

        Of other outposts of the former parish of
Blackburn, Bamber Bridge and Cuerden are stuck close
to the new M6 and show off acres of new housing and
occasional mill and church silhouettes. Great Harwood
is more interesting and has a medieval parish church
as well as its own town hall of 1900 along with other
public buildings. The settlement also contains what
is regarded as a fascinating old house, Marholme,
which includes late medieval, Elizabethan and
Jacobean work and is something of a showpiece.

        Early directories point to the booming economy
of Blackburn as responsible for so much change.
Cotton was providing work c1650 , it is recorded, but
it was the 1760s which witnessed a dramatic expansion of
cotton trade. In later decades further inventions
of new machinery further enhanced the industrial
expansion, with more and bigger mills, and above all
in the 1820s when cotton spinning (as opposed to the
making of cotton materials) was mechanised thoroughly.

        The result of the growth of cotton was that
in the 1820s it was confidently asserted that
10,000 out of the population were employed in the
several branches of the cotton industry - or nearly one
half of the entire population ! Nowadays the workforce
is employed in industries which are rather more
broadly based !

OLDHAM

        Beside me are two pictures of Oldham, once
the supreme example of a cotton mill town: one
picture is of an aerial view of the town in 1936
showing many tall chimneys and industrial premises,
the other is an aerial view of the same district
taken in 1989, with all of the chimneys gone and most
of the industrial premises too. Change is that
devastating, just as it must have been in the 18th
and 19th centuries when cotton boomed.

        Oldham's population in the 1730s was charted
as about 8,000, and it rose to 9,500 about 1792,
12,000 by 1801, and 22,000 in 1821. This was a series
of startling increases: the whole parish itself
had 21,000 in 1801 and 38,000 by 1821, for it covered
the considerable townships of Chadderton and Crompton
as well as the chapelry of Royton. Oldham lies
between Ashton in the south and Rochdale in the north,
and is trapped against the Pennines by the growth of
Manchester to the south west. It remains a big town,
and from the climbing hillsides one gets good views
across the town and its neighbours.

        Strictly speaking of course Oldham was not in
the 1820s even a parish, for it still was classed as
a chapel of ease to the parish church of Prestwich,
8 miles away: spectacular growth here as in the other
industrial towns had left the old ecclesiastical

system hopelessly outdated. The result was that the
curate at Oldham had one church in which to house
all that population ! It was no wonder that the other,
rival denominations did so well: Quakers, Congregationalists,
Wesleyan and Primitive (and later other) Methodists,
Baptists, Unitarians and even Moravians - anyone seems
to have flourished in that free for all chapelry and
township.

Local government too was utterly inadequate:
how the parish vestry at Prestwich managed to control
with any degree of efficiency affairs for a place of
40,000 defies the imagination !

Oldham's industrial importance came from its
coal, its wool and above all cotton, for out of
65 cotton mills at work in the town in the 1820s
63 were products of the 19th century's first two
decades. At the same time there were 140 steam engines
and increasing numbers of chimneys belching out smoke
and other effluvia - washing must have been a serious
headache ! There were a large number of collieries too
and vast amounts of this and cotton products were sent out
by packhorse, canal and later railways, often first to
Manchester for resale.

SOUTHPORT

I spent my childhood and youth within an easy
trip to this resort, famous for its vast acreage of
sand and sand dunes, its vistas of remote sea, its great
flower show, the shopping, hotels and much more. In
recent years it has become something of a Merseyside
extension, but it retains a genteel flavour and allows
its many visitors to amble along flat routes which do not
tax even the worst heart condition ! The famous subsiding
landscape has thrown up various strangely bent houses too,
which one still occasionally comes across.

Historically it is a new town in the very best of
traditions: it was a smattering of fishing cottages until
Mr Sutton of North Meols decided to build an hotel in
1792, and by the 1800s it was enjoying trade thanks to the
vicissitudes of European travel in the French Wars (the
Lake District also benefited). There were a dozen hotels
of varying types and 200 houses by the 1820s, with brick
the favoured building material. The entertainments were
decidedly spartan: walking, drinking, newsroom, library,
and above all the 40 and more bathing machines dragged
each day into the reluctant seascape for the benefit
of modesty and health.

From a parish of 2,000 the place grew to 3,000
in 20 years, and by the 1860s 10,000 with that many again
as tourists - and usually of the middling sort, neither the
well off nor the poor people . In the 1960s, the decade of
my most memorable visits, it was 80,000 and endless queues
of day trippers.

The town appears to have been regularly planned, with many wide and straight streets, lots of trees to soften the townscape, excellent pavements, and a fine set of open spaces ranging from gardens and parks to beach and promenade. It is the churches which strike one about the buildings - like most such resorts it was heavily evangelical and Nonconformist, so that the religious historian would have a fieldday in the archives.

Christ Church of 1820 was the first place of worship, a chapel of ease in the new town and since then much expanded. From the 1870s there was constant church building into the 1910s - St Luke, Emmanuel, St Andrew, numerous late Victorian and Edwardian Methodist, Congregational and Presbyterian chapels for the affluent offcomers who came in ever greater numbers thanks to efficient railways and the pull of the resort of a retirement home well away from south Lancashire, Manchester, and other towns' greyness.

Thanks to William Atkinson, the rich Preston cotton manufacturer, came the gift of a fine library and town art gallery prominently situated in 1870s Lord Street. The original town hall was of the 1850s and served a small resort: on a majestic scale however is the long pier, haunt of my youth, and one of the longest in the country - it needs to be with the sea so far out ! Everyone used to joke that you could not drown if you jumped off the end of Southport pier ! You broke your neck instead on the sand.

Of the green bits, Hesketh park is the Victorian showpiece complete with lake and ducks, charming lodges, a large fern conservatory that acknowledges how cheap fuel was in 1900, and animals. Up at the poshest part of the town, Churchtown, which people still call their village, are the equally pleasant Botanic Gardens. I once bought a history of the Southport lifeboat crews from the museum in one of the parks, written and printed in 1949 and still on sale in the 1970s for its original price of 1 shilling !

Churchtown too has the oldest place of worship - St Cuthbert's, a fine building of the 1730s: nearby too the old inns, the Bold Arms and the Hesketh Arms, reflecting the names of the principal landowners of the district.

We used to go to Southport for the air: vast quantities of wind in winter left the streets amazingly quiet, and then there was the shopping after bargains in some of the finest shops of the region. The great Wayfarers Arcade always attracted us, and who could forget its upstairs openair cafe, its distinctive shops, decorations, pond and flowers, all sheltered in the February halfterm from the biting winds. The hotels are a formidable array: the Royal Clifton, the Prince of Wales, the Queens, the Victoria and others. One always had to walk what seemed to be vast distances to get to the little (and odiferous) zoo where we fed the animals de rigueur before sampling the fairground and its thrills.

Outer Southport includes Birkdale and Ainsdale, two very prosperous suburbs of vast extent heightened by the flatness of the landscape. Enormous numbers of Edwardian, interwar and modern housing, in no way as attractive as the town centre.

Southport above all was built to cater for consumption: that is, the consumer with money to burn: hence the array of shops, eating places and premises for unloading oneself of the burden of money ! Interestingly in the 1960s it boasted about the best pet shop and the finest bookshop in the district, and we used to come especially for these reasons for many years. I should mention the time we bought 4 foot grass snakes which escaped in the car on the way home and terrorised ..... but that is quite enough personal information: historically Southport is a Victorian holiday resort which remains full of pleasure.

FLEETWOOD

HASLINGDEN

Fleetwood sits uneasily along the coast north of Blackpool and ever under the shadow of its enormous neighbour. The town of course is characterised by being flat and having extensive port and harbour districts. In 1830 the district was simply sand and marsh, but in typical improving fashion, the local squire decided to create a major resort, town and port in the 1830s with the help of the railways.

Sir Peter Hesketh Fleetwood actually ruined himself in the process of giving birth to Fleetwood: Decimus Burton, a prominent and famous architect and planner, was employed to lay out the town plan and to design a number of fine buildings which were to grace the urban scene. A railway was completed by 1840 to link the place to Preston and hence the industrial midlands, Yorkshire and south Lancashire, and buildings such as the North Euston hotel and the Queens Terrace were designed and erected.

Fleetwood's home now houses the famous Rossall public school, founded in 1844 and mainly looking like great red brick boxes. It is big, and gave work to the Lancaster firm of Austin and Paley (two generations of each name) for some years - they were a well known and highly original firm from Lancaster. The port is chiefly known for its deepwater fishing fleet, the fine old lighthouse some way inland, and great swathes of grass and gardens exposed to the sea breezes. A little ferry (which I used to use) crosses the Wyre to tiny Knot End .

Haslingden was one of the many townships and chapelries within the great medieval parish of Whalley which survived on wool and cloth throughout the centuries. Architecturally the town is regarded as bereft of interest by the authorities, but it has its Georgian parish church of St James complete with later additions, several large nonconformist chapels, and the countryside to add interest alongside the modern housing and the various mills and industrial premises of varying ages.

Haslingden experienced the rapid growth which affected even so small a place - 4,000 population at the first census but towards 7,000 in the 1820s with the consequent building boom, mill work and so on. It was all wool and woollen products into the later 18th century, but then cotton arrived - that brash newcomer whose millowners adapted so much better than the wool men to the new inventions of the day, and cotton triumphed in the course of the Victorian years.

There is to be seen in directories of the day the usual run of attornies and academies, butchers and tailors, cloggers and smiths: interesting are the lists of wool carders and scribblers, 17 cotton manufacturers, a dozen cotton spinners, and above all 29 flannel manufacturers. The same names occur again and again - 4 Ashworths, 4 Haworths, 4 Stotts for instance. The directory shows the vast youthfulness of the population too: 1400 out of 6,500 attended the Sunday schools in the 1820s. How age structure has changed !

DARWEN

Darwen was typical of the many out-townships
of Lancashire which suddenly found themselves growing
by leaps and bounds thanks to the industrial revolution.
Divided into Over and Lower Darwen, the village was
simply a township of the enormous parish of Blackburn,
that rarity of towns in being both a parish and comprising
more or less the entire Hundred. Coal was for many
decades dug locally in Darwen, and by the 1800s there
were jobs to be had in the print works (for material),
the bleaching establishments, and in the several slate
quarries. Cotton ruled throughout the 19th and 20th
centuries, and the population was towards 30,000 by
the 1960s.

As was usual in such places, the Church of
England was weak and the Nonconformists (or Dissenters)
very strong. Thomas Rickman's parish church of Holy
Trinity, despite its being by the Commissioners responsible
for church building (at a time when church accommodation
was desperately lacking in industrial districts) and having
copious galleries, could not stand the pace of Dissenting
provision. Thus substantial Baptist, Methodist and
Congregational chapels, several Roman Catholic ones (for
the Irish who worked in the bleach works etc), and not
much else.

The town has town hall and library, a few
good late Georgian properties, but the real star is the
India Mills of the 1860s built for cotton spinning by
the firm of Shorrock Brothers and the principal employment
at one time. The family of Shorrock had various
properties and several mills and business premises in
this working town, and the skyline showed off their
chimneystacks at each place - one as high as 300 feet.

In the 1820s the place was well supplied with
chapels and with 15 or 20 public houses. The directories
list the assorted bleach works, quarries, coal mines,
cotton mills, and the occupations in smaller numbers.

Today Darwen remains a giant village at heart.
I might mention too that in Sunnyhurst Wood the town has
an enviable beauty spot complete with excellent visitors'
centre: well done !

NELSON

Nelson is one of the big villages which were created as Lancashire grew into an industrial giant in the 19th century. During the 18th century industry grew up here in Nelson in the shape of cotton mills, using the good road from Blackburn into Yorkshire and in time the big Leeds - Liverpool canal also. A string of mills and other industries grew up, at first on a modest scale, then later rebuilt larger, during the Victorian years, and the product was a shapeless sprawl of buildings which this century has done nothing to improve !

I once had to go for a business meeting to the town and, it being my first visit, I explored on foot: but there really was little to see except the hills beyond. Plenty of Victorian chapels and churches remain. In spite of the good road, Nelson retains a remote atmosphere throughout the years. One can certainly imagine the Pendle witches at large, and there is an excellent Pendle Heritage centre in nearby Barrowford which deals with the whole district. The town emerged from the twin Marsden villages in the middle ages, and with booming wool by the 17th century, the town developed: the new cotton trade transformed it all.

Since my first visits Nelson has gained a big new shopping centre, making it even more town-like.

Colne is yet another of those Pennine moorside parishes which grew large thanks to the industrial revolution but which remain villages at heart. In Colne's case, the settlement follows along a valley floor and sides: the swift flowing streams and river provided power for the woollen mills and industries into the 19th century, by which time cotton was king here as in so many places in Lancashire. The rapid development of cotton firms meant that the population of 3,000 in the 1790s had grown to over 7,000 in the 1820s - but such growth could not be sustained, and into the 1960s it was only 19,000 or so.

It is funny what one recalls about places: on my first visit to Colne a helpful local told me of the occurrence in 1777 when the gallery collapsed in the Methodist meeting house when John Wesley himself was preaching to a multitude: it was one of those disasters which are so rare in one small town that it was recalled as if it had been yesterday.

Architecturally one must not expect too much: the big parish church of St Batholomew is mostly restored medieval, mainly 15th century and later with 13th century bits and pieces. It was much repaired in 1815 after it threatened to collapse. There are the usual public buildings like town hall and municipal hall, a clutch of big Dissenting chapels, and a

proud tradition of Inghamite places of worship (rare
survivals in the county exist of other Inghamite
churches, socalled after their founder, Wesley's erstwhile
friend and colleague, Benjamin Ingham).

The star in the history of Colne was of course
the great wool hall, apparently one to rival that at
Halifax. It measured 170 feet by 55 feet, was of
23 bays with a fine five bay pediment at the entrance,
and was used by the wool trade and merchants for their
business. It was paid for by subscribers, after the
fashion of the day, and put up in 1775. However wool
went into decline, mainly thanks to cotton, and the
great hall became a general market and business
hall. It was neglected and eventually demolished:
what a blow for the town.

One can certainly find out about the local
history of Colne from the Pendle Heritage centre or
the local tourist information centres. Not far away
are various interesting villages including picturesque
Newchurch with an interesting old church, and
the little mining museum at Earby. Nearer to the town
is the most unusual British in India museum.

BACUP

Bacup is one of those small towns which seem to
have been passed by so far as the written word is
concerned. It is hard to find much out about it, for it
is simply a township in the middle ages and into the
19th century of the great parish of Whalley. Directories
make little of it, and a visit to it is not that
enlightening. It is a place which (as so many in this
area did) had both woollen and cotton manufacturers,
with cotton eventually prevailing and taking over the
mills. The directories mention the names of some of the
mills: Dogpits, Greave, Haddock End, Flours, now mostly
gone or altered beyond recognition. There is the
usual large number of Victorian places of worship for
many denominations - plenty of public houses too are
listed ! No lack of detached villas for the better off
and the professional families and manufacturers, and
lots of dreary rows for the workforce in little terraced
properties on the hillsides.

Scattered around the valleys are some interesting
places for the tourist. The little town has a natural
history museum and the unique Pennine Aviation museum;
a way out of town down at Whitworth is the local
history museum which is a selfhelp affair and most
creditable - its exhibits would also stand for Bacup,
the two being so close and similar socially and
economically. Though I have not seen it, there is an
astronomy centre not far out of town too, of all things !

ACCRINGTON

ASHTON UNDER LYNE

My first recollection of Accrington concerns the dismal fate of its soccer league team, Accrington Stanley some years ago, when one of my early teachers bemoaned his home town's soccer fate as it left the league forever ! It was a large village in the 18th century but just one of scores of townships or chapelries under the aegis of Whalley. Amongst the principal industrial concerns were the calico printing works of Robert Peel and others from the third quarter of the 18th century: thereafter cotton mills and allied trades flourished, brought in people, and led to the building of many terraces of little houses for the millworkers.

One would not expect such a little town to have much in the way of good architecture: it was a big village of around 3,000 people in the 1800s, over 18,000 in the 1860s and over 40,000 in the 1900s (though it stagnated thereafter) and this is a large town by Victorian standards. There are the usual collection of Anglican, Methodist, Congregational and other churches, plus the town hall of the 1850s which was built to acknowledge the debt of the town to the Peel family as major benefactors to the town. It shows off the money available in its rusticated stonework - one would go a long way to find such extravagance in many smaller towns of the county ! The main Anglican church was St James, dating from the 1760s but several times enlarged as money and population pressure required. The changes in vista and hillsides are welcome. Do not miss the art gallery which is not only housed in a fine old building but shows off superb glass including Tiffany glass.

One of the more ancient settlements of the county and with some prominence in county affairs, Ashton had a population of around 5,000 in the 1770s which had grown thanks to the cotton industry to over 20,000 by the 1820s. Plenty of swift flowing streams including the river Tame (hence the modern administrative name) , lots of coal within a couple of miles, and a good blend of modern canals with reasonable roads encouraged cotton: as every schoolchild doing GCSE social and economic history could add, the wet weather made handling difficult cotton thread all that much easier !

The first time I visited the town was for a wedding, and it struck me then and on subsequent trips that it was a true industrial town stuck between the back of Manchester and the Pennines: lots of smoke and dirt blackened buildings, mills and other industrial buildings, endless terraced houses, and the obvious impact of rail and road and canal.

The Asshetons were the big local family, and hence one supposes the eponymous town. They were reasonably prominent in national affairs, fighting in all the right medieval and Wars of the Roses battles, in the Civil Wars of the 1640s, and (as with so many local families) had divided loyalties therein: it was prudent to so do from the point of view of keeping one's estates.

Coal used to be found in some quantities hereabouts:
also used for centuries was the peat cut from Ashton
Moss, a quaking or shaking bog of the sort commonly found
on unimproved land and nowadays of special scientific
value now that so few still exist. Was peat used in
the many steam engines in the mills ? Presumably not since
its calorific value is so much lower. The heyday of
the cotton firms involved in spinning fine yarn for the
weaving of fine ginghams, calicoes and muslins was the
1780s to the 1860s, though it took a long time for
an appreciable decline to set in.

Directories list the usual host of cotton
manufacturers and spinners: several Higginbothams,
Reyners plus assorted Cromptons (there's a name !)
Leighs, Orrells and many others. There used to be a
number of outtownships or villages under the parish in
which mills too flourished, and including Lees,
Medlock, Woodhouses and Knott Lanes, all more or less
swallowed in Victorian and modern times into the main
conurbation. As one would expect, Dissent flourished,
and my old history professor made a study of the many
schools, both day and Sunday, to be found packed with
children avid for learning in the 19th century.

The buildings and townscape are very much a
creation of the dramatic industrial revolution involving
coal and cotton.

CARNFORTH

Carnforth hardly figures in the pages of Lancashire
history thanks to its being a small village within the
parish of Warton in North Lancs and just by the present
Cumbrian boundary and M6. It was a bit of a staging
post on the last lap to Kendal in the 18th and early 19th
centuries, and hence the Joiners Arms, Malt Shovel and
Golden Ball having facilities for changing horses with
their ostlers in attendance - it would have been in place
for young Boz (or Dickens) in the 1830s too. There was
also the Lancaster to Kendal section of the canal from
Preston, the one beloved of so many boaters since it has
not a single lock but simply occasional little swing
bridges - and now grievously damaged by the M6. We used
to attend the canal each spring for a week's sojourn,
walking in the rain from the tow path past dingy canalside
buildings to the local shops.

What changed the town - in fact made the place
into a town - was the arrival of the railway lines from
Carlisle and Scotland to the north on the way south, and
from Barrow (also a, larger, rail town) down the valley
to Settle and Yorkshire. From then onwards sleepiness
was swept aside in the rail boom, and a large iron works
using haematite ores which required plentiful limestone
to be had locally grew up to help furnish the iron and
steel needs of the rail companies. A famous railway
museum graces the town today, plus substantial amounts of
later Victorian and modern council and private housing.

GRANGE OVER SANDS

The most genteel of resorts, this one, now just inside Cumbria thanks to the atrocities of 1974, but firmly historically part of Lancashire. It was a small village which had its farmers and fisherfolk when it attracted tourists and visitors in the early 19th century mainly attracted by the superb scenery and mild climate. Mrs Gaskell, the doyen of Manchester literary circles in the 1840s, holidayed locally and found all charming if utterly primitive.

What happened to the village was the railway from Carnforth to Barrow in Furness, also an 1840s hamlet which burgeoned under the impact of iron, steel, ship building and above all the iron mines and railways of the district. The navvies ruthlessly hacked through the apparently elysian woods and plonked the present rail embankment for miles along the coast and foreshore cutting off the town from the sea. That was in the mid 1850s, and though growth was in fits and starts, the place was deliberately developed as a small but posh resort with its grand hotels, views, and plentiful terraced houses.

Baths for example , fine hotels, the graceful promenade and parks, are all tastefully provided: but not much else even today, and the locals intend to understate and undersell the town.

Not much in the way of history: I recall a nice little history and a learned thesis on the place, and everything is most picturesque - but not much else ! The parish church of the 1850s was repeatedly extended so that it seems to have endless aisles and a little knolly site - and no lack of other, Dissenting, churches too. One notices the pleasant clock tower as it impedes and divides traffic, the great Grange and Grand hotels, the very attractive Netherwood (formerly the country home for the Dakins of Bolton and of superb quality), and the big former convalescent home and school of unsuitable brick. Odd corners provide glimpses of old Grange - several cottages by the main centre car park, others near the station. The woods come right down the hill to intermingle with the new housing which reaches right up to the heights - I always wonder why so many retired folk come here to live when it steep gradients (even up from the promenade) must play havoc with heart, chest and arthritic conditions !

ST HELENS

I often wonder how many of my fellows, at schools
in this town in the 1960s, remain in it today: like me,
most if not all from the old grammar seem to have flown the
coop.   It is an unloved and unlovable place from many
points of view, with endless grimy terraces of poor
housing, black industrial buildings with infamous chimneys
sending out noxious odours and vapours , and no proper
boundaries as it merges into neighbouring towns in one
great conurbation of traffic and townscape of the least
attractive types. Harsh words from an old son ? Yes,
but deserved.

St Helens of course was a chapel of ease and
small settlement in the big parish of Prescot, which
came to prominence in the 19th century thanks to the
growth of glass, coal and other industries which led to
the merging into one amorphous whole of the former old
villages of Eccleston, Bold, Parr, Sutton and others -
their old halls and buildings nearly all gone too.
3,000 people c1800, upto 5,000 in the 1820s, and by
the 1960s well over 100,000.

In the 1770s the glass industry came of age with
the establishment of the large Ravenhead British Plate
glass company with some hundreds of employees using the
local white Sherdley sand and coal. An extensive copper
industry grew up too from the same decade and led to the
importing of lots of Welsh workers; by the 1820s, and
especially in the 1840s, it was the Roman Catholic Irish
who flocked in their thousands to work in the chemical
firms, endangering their health and lives but gaining
a living and making St Helens into the most Catholic of
Lancashire towns.   Not only various noxious chemical
firms, plus any number of pottery and glass firms,
were established in the late 18th and early 19th
centuries, but also came into being Beachams, the famous
pill firm right in the town centre along with great clock
tower (and smells).   ONe Beacham of course became
the well known music conductor but the firm continues.

As well known are Pilkingtons, the king of the
glass world and furnishing millionaires in the family in
this century. I recall old Sir Harry bicycling from
his Windle Hall into the town (only a mile or two) as
he passed us schoolboys on unwelcome cross country
fatigues: the family were strong Congregationalists
for many years, and their pensioners were always the best
cared for in the town.

Outsiders associate the town with pills, glass
and coal, though there has long been the famous brewery
of Greenalls and in this century a plethora of light
industrial development. In the last 20 years many of the
Victorian properties have made way for new shopping
centres and the like, but there remain enough to give a
good idea of what St Helens was and is: a working town.
Gems stay in the memory: Taylor and Victoria Parks,
Cowley House, the 17th century Quaker meetinghouse,
the big Pilkington glass museum and their HQ in brashest
1960s style, the old town hall in Victoria Square.
And of course the rugby league and rugby at the schools
retains its mass support. The famous racing driver
Geoff Duke was a local lad and had a garage down the
road from my school. Ah ! memories ! One also recalls the
ghastly smells down Merton Bank, cesspool streams and
poisoned places we were told to avoid: environmentalists
would still have a field day in the town !

KIRKHAM

DALTON IN FURNESS

        Until the growth of Victorian Barrow, Dalton
was the principal town of the whole North Lancashire
area across the Sands. It retains, high up on the
elevated land, the big, proud Paley and Austin
parish church with recent expensive additions and fine
site, dating from the 1880s and mostly paid for by the
all-powerful duke of Devonshire and his family, the
Cavendishes of Holker Hall nearby (and many other
stately homes across the country). Near to the parish church
are the Georgian quarters, a smattering of larger and
smaller houses showing a modest prosperity and with
the castle in the centre. This actually is a large pele,
now a museum, and offering good views from the top of
its 45 by 30 foot walls.

        In reality there is not much to detain the
tourist: any number of Victorian terraces from the
days of heady expansion in the iron ore mines locally,
plus lots of churches and chapels brought by the
migrants from Cornwall, Devon, the midlands, Scotland,
Ireland and so on. Once this happened, Barrow became the
main town for work, but Ulverston beckoned as chief
residential district for the affluent of Furness and
Cartmel in the 19th century. Dalton was left to become
very working class ! It now seems simply an adjunct to
Barrow down the road and the glories of Furness abbey.

        Kirkham is the main centre in the flat country
between Blackpool and Preston: it enjoys the distinction
of having been the scene of my first motoring breakdown
in my own car and the garage charged the collosal sum of
£25 for a new gearbox and fitting ! They also would
not release the car except for cash ! However it is now
a much extended residential place, handy for both
large towns and for the M6. Its main historical
importance was ever as a market centre, which it
continues to be, and for being head of an extensive parish
covering 13 townships and 5 chapelries. In fact most
of the modern admin unit of Wyre was under Kirkham's
church sway.

        The directories show plenty of the usual
industries - butchers, bakers, tailors, metal trades,
drapers, a dozen inns and pubs, and the whole gamut
of the small town economy. Of more interest is the
waterborne trade as vessels from the Baltic brought in
their wares in the 18th and early 19th centuries:
merchants had warehouses on the Wyre a few miles to the
north, and brought the raw materials by road to be
turned into sail cloth, ropes, and various sorts of
linen. There was cotton too, even here, remote from east
Lancashire: Birley's cotton mill was the principal cotton
place for years, and it was long hoped (forlornly as it
transpired) that a canal would be cut to the Lancaster one
 near Treales.

Architecturally the town is not in the least notable. The parish church of St Michael's had to be entirely rebuilt in 1822 at a considerable cost of £5,000 raised solely by levying a church rate on a minority of the parish. Bearing in mind the unpopularity of the modern new taxation, one can imagine what was said about this at the time ! The Roman Catholic church is said to be one of A W Pugin's, but I found it uninspiring and not a patch on the little gem at Warwick Bridge in Cumberland of the same date, c1843.

There are some interesting cottages and odd terraces, and the town grammar school buildings are regarded as good designs too.

GARSTANG

As we chugged along the Lancaster canal it was the aqueduct which carried the water over the little river Wyre which signalled the arrival of our entourage in the pleasant little town of Garstang. Today it is very much a commuter town, serving Lancaster, Preston and Blackpool and with housing prices very high indeed; but it is an ancient market town, once a very extensive parish, and in the 1820s with only a population of 1,000 out of a parish total of over 7,000.

Economically speaking the town was more or less dependent on the agricultural business of the district, its market, and good position on the A6, catching both coaching trade and modern tourists. There used to be some small mills involved in cotton trade, whilst the directories present the common picture of a small regional town at its height c1780-c1830. The canal also helped, and it is easy to underestimate its importance in the same period.

Architecturally there is absolutely nothing to impress, but there is an air of charm about the place: a miniscule town hall turned into shops, a mid 18th century market cross, Rennie's fine aqueduct of the 1790s, a bit of remains for Greenhalgh castle which played its part in affairs into the 17th century. The main street, depite narrow pavements, runs on into the distance and invites inspection.

E G Paley of Lancaster designed the uninspiring
but large RC church of the 1850s shortly after the
retirement of his partner and mentor Edmund Sharpe, and
there is both a Congregational and Methodist chapel.
St Thomas, the Anglican chapel in the town itself,
is a typical product of the periods: a nave and west
tower of 1770, and a rebuilt chancel of the 1870s when
liturgical and high church changes demanded something better
than a stumpy Georgian one. The parish church is
towards two miles away in Churchtown, or Kirkland.
There remains at this church of St Helen a good deal of
13th century masonry, and the parish was of course in
the hands of not too distant Cockersands abbey for most of
the middle ages . Considerable changes took place to the
fabric in the 15th, 16th and later centuries.

St Helen was at the centre of the parish of
course, not offset in Garstang township, and hence its
remoteness - and the success of other denominations in
what would seem to be an unpromising field.

Garstang today thrives on tourism and prosperous
commuters: it has a good balance of old back street
businesses and brash new boutique type shops. It remains
right by the river, canal and open country - I remember
swimming in the Wyre as a student - and the quality of life
is high. Historically it was small but interesting in
a quiet way.

HEYSHAM

Heysham is one of those large villages or small
towns which have been completely taken over by their
overweening neighbour (in this case Morecambe), and
despite modern urban growth it is still possible to
find a distinct gap between the two on maps before
1970. There is far more older property than in the
neighbouring giant, and Heysham has for centuries been
one of the smaller county parishes and, strangely,
without any townships or villages outside itself.

The church of St Peter's shows off its
Anglo-Saxon history, and there are parts of the early
Norman work on display in the sort of primitive and
coarse garb to be expected wherever there was lack of
money or skill as in such a backwater c1100. An
interesting church for the archaeologist and the tourist,
and Morecambe has nothing to compare.

And up the hill is St Patrick's, an almost
totally Saxon chapel of the 8th or 9th centuries,
and of consuming interest too, though only small. There are
in the vicinity of the churches some Georgian properties
including the Middleton Arms. We used to frequent the
local hostleries on tedious Sundays when most of the
place was closed. If you go, do not miss the
Half Moon Battery with its views and cannons, or the walks
hereabouts. Heysham of course now is a harbour and a
power station , but there is a long history of seabathing
by the genteel classes before the railway created rivals.

ULVERSTON

This ancient Lancashire North of the Sands market town at one time included within its compass a good deal of the lakeland scenery including Coniston. Prominent landowners have included the great Cistercian abbey at Furness, the Braddylls and the Cavendishes: it was a prosperous medieval town which like so many was mainly rebuilt and much enlarged in the rich decades of the 18th and early 19th centuries - it also   benefited from the coming of the railways and growth of Furness ore mining, the 1790s canal into the estuary which allowed a small industrial centre near its terminus, and from an influx of the wealthy from Victorian Barrow.

Its population was 3,000 in the 1800s, over 5,000 in the 1830s, and it is today besieged at times by tourists - but not too many most of the year; for it remains happily just outside the lakeland orbit and serves its widely scattered population still. Lots of wool trade, some cotton products, plenty of ore transport, wood and woodland tradestuff such as baskets, hoops. charcoal and of course stone for roofing and building. This wealth, especially c1780-c1830, created the sort of provincial culture which had a mechanics institute, libraries, savings bank, theatre and town hall quite early for this remote district.

Architecturally it should be viewed as a whole, not with an idea to important buildings - of which there are none in the town centre.

The star is Conishead Priory, built in utterly splendid and extravagant fashion between 1821 and 1836 and which bankrupted the Braddylls - who were only middling gentry, too poor for this palace. Philip Wyatt was the designer, and provided a vast Gothic show of turrets, towers, spires, gatehouse, vast areas of plasterwork, gallery, screens and so on. All restored recently by the religious community now in residence, and open to the public.

St Mary's the parish church, is a total disappointment, for its old bits are added on to a fierce and unsympathetic 1860s rebuild by Paley (without the skill of his later partner Austin) to provide a big empty preaching box. The Commissioners church of St Mary, by Salvin, c1830, is out of use; several large Dissenting places of worship too. But enjoy a walkabout down Market Street, Market Place, Union and Fountain Streets, and look at the old shops, houses and offices so chastely provided in the 18th century - many now being nicely restored.

Conishead of course was a small Augustinian priory in the middle ages, until replaced by a modest country house in the 17th century and the gigantic one of the 19th. The sea and coast are nearby, as are several worthy village churches and the lakeland scenery. The town remains well worth an inspection, but it must be on foot - no vehicles offer any sort of advantage here.

BARROW IN FURNESS

A few score people lived in the remote hamlet
of Barrow in Furness in the 1830s, but it was to be
transformed into one of the most dynamic of towns in
the next 5 decades thanks to the industrial revolution
associated with iron, steel, railways and mining.
Barrow owes its prominence in so unpromising a site to
the vast iron ore deposits discovered by Schneider
about 1840. With his partner, the Scot Robert Hannay, W H
Schneider not only found the ores but exported them in
increasing quantities in various unrefined and
refined states, and took a prominent part in the life of
the new town and port of his creation. The real architect
of the town was James Ramsden, a railway manager but soon
in favour with the two great landowners the dukes of
Devonshire and of Buccleuch (Devonshire lived at Holker
for much of the year). Thanks to Ramsden the town was
planned, properly built and given novelties such as
proper sewers and water supply - though errors were made,
and much housing was appalling from the very start in
the boom conditions like the wild west of the USA.

The population was still only 3,000 in 1861,
but 19,000 in 1871 and 47,000 10 years later, making it
the largest town between Preston and Glasgow. Population
peaked at 74,000 in 1921, but that masked the problems
of industrial decline which had bedevilled the town
and its promoters for decades. It now plays second
fiddle to Carlisle within Cumbria.

Those who have read the many works of J D
Marshall will know of the town's history, its great
iron and steel plants, its jute works, the shipbuilding
and armaments factory which still flourishes, and of the
gradual town improvement schemes needed to cope with the
swelling migrants. Tourists are rare to Barrow, as one
might expect in so uncompromisingly a working town: yet
the planned centre is worth a look, there are the
spectacular ruins of Furness abbey next door, and
a number of good walks.

The first parish church was that of St
George c1860 and designed by E G Paley - pleasant and
cost effective, people would say today: it was home to
the notorious ritualist clergyman T S Barrett, who
missioned the slums and helped so many folk who lacked
education and health facilities. St James, a few years
later, has fine spire, polygonal apse and coloured
brick to show off: there are other parish churches too
as provision for worship for the migrants was the principal
concern of the bosses and landowners who never thought to
provide for public health, schools and so on till later.

An excellent set of Dissenting churches too
including great Methodist, Congregational and
Presbyterian ones: the Roman Catholics employed
E W Pugin to create a small cathedral.

I suppose the peak of prosperity is shown in
the big town hall of the 1880s, full of civic
pride and consciousness that Barrow had arrived: it
was recently made a borough and returned its own MP.
Remarkably, MPs in so poor a place were often Tory !
For the student of social, economic and political
history Barrow provides much - including a clutch of
theses and learned articles.

MORECAMBE

Morecambe began life in the late 1840s after the arrival of the railway (that most revolutionary form of transport) that transformed a hamlet into a town and resort. There is little that is not late Victorian or 20th century in the town, and one has to look hard for anything of architectural merit. Historically the town always depended on tourism, and by the 1960s the horde of boarding house owners were saved from decline (due to the overseas boom) thanks to the opportunities to let to several thousand Lancaster university and college students.

One problem for the town has been that it is very flat so that landscaping value is lost. The town hall is the showpiece in its fine gardens, and there are several parks and lots of grass and room - especially with a promenade stretching nearly 5 miles. Yet I recall endless rows of bungalows on the back roads, of big terraced houses near the centre, no decent buildings at all to alleviate boring bus journeys on Sundays as students looked for "action" !

What are now submerged former rural outposts at Bare and Torrisholme do have some 17th and 18th century cottages and houses with occasional datestones on display - but just look at the post 1920 housing sea ! The pubs and hotels stand out. The Midland Hotel above all is a showpiece, of the 1930s and beautifully restored in recent years to its former glory so that it could shine in a recent TV series set in its birth decade. Its sweeping curves to seaward and landward, elegant staircase and balconies, show of the quality - othersjust follow.

The town hall is a vaguely classical design of the 1930s. The parish church of Holy Trinity is one of Edmund Sharpe's designs of the 1840s - fine roof and tower structures here. St Barnabas is by his succesors in the firm , Austin and Paley and of the 1890s, and St Christopher's is a 1930s design by the firm near the end of its life. As one would expect in such a resort, there are a plethora of Dissenting churches, mainly Victorian with a few modern ones. I remember attending several churches in the town: the Methodist one in Torrisholme, a 1960s edifice, had standing room only. One old chap fell asleep and could not be wakened up, so he had to be carried over heads and to the fresh air where he recovered ! How many of the churches are thus packed now ?

One cannot miss the piers: we spent many hours on them at the end of the season and before they closed for the winter. Central and West End piers they were called, and the walk between them to see which was open in November was a long slog against the chilling wind.

Morecambe today is a resort before it is anything else, and it offers its many delights and pleasures for visitors to unburden themselves of their cash in much the same way as Blackpool and others. Historically it loses out to Lancaster, with whom it is now united as an administrative unit, but as an example of resort development it provides interesting comment on the period 1850-1950.

LANCASTER

One can only know a town by living in it, but despite my three years at Lancaster I must admit to never having got to know it as intimately as I should have done. It is nowadays twinned with its new partner Morecambe, but two such dissimilar towns could hardly be imagined though they are both of a size. Lancaster is the old capital of a large county, but it remains one of the middling to small centres in a county of big urban districts. It had a population of 9,000 within the city itself (but 17,000 in the actual parish of Lancaster) in 1801 and 10,000 (or nearly 20,000) in the 1820s (in the 1970s it was 50-odd thousand). Lancaster was an important Roman station though the extent of its importance needs much investigation, rather like that of Carlisle. The town became of new importance during the early Norman days, and remained so for centuries.

Architecturally speaking the town is especially fortunate in having so many hills and such splendid opportunities denied Morecambe (we always hoped to break down in Morecambe was hopeless if one's battery was flat !). - Up on the castle hill the actual castle has long been an important gaol, though I hear that this function will shortly cease. The castle is Norman but the medieval core is heavily overlaid by 18th and 19th century alterations, plus the usual 16th century strengthening against cannon and the Scots. The castle too houses the shire hall

since the rebuilding c1800 to J M Gandy's designs. I recall the museum with its delightful (!) condemned cell and noose room - all very evocative of the good old days. Lancaster remains with its courts, and over the centuries there have been many famous trials including those of the 1600s Lancashire witches.

The finest church of the town is of course the former Benedictine priory of St Mary's up by the castle, and built on a Roman and Saxon site. The new foundation of the 1090s meant that it was an alien priory under a foreign House, and when this was politically unacceptable in the wars with France it (with many others) was taken off the foreigners and given to someone else c1414. The church exhibits Saxon, Norman and later medieval masonry and the woodwork is especially fine - it seems to have come from either Furness or Cockersands monastery. Altogether one of the most satisfactory of the monastic remains of the county.

What one comes to see in Lancaster is the large amount of Georgian architecture which makes the place so notable.

There are several famous Georgian buildings. One is the old town hall of the early 1780s complete with great Tuscan portico, smooth rusticated (expensive indeed !) stonework and cupola with rotunda and Ionic colums. This is now the town museum and devotes itself to the town's industries, social history and so on. In nice contrast is the cottage museum at 15 Castle Hill, a 1730s building which has been totaly refurbished as an artisan's family home from the 1820s - and what a good job was done too ! In regard to places of worship there are both Anglican and Dissenting from the Georgian years, and fine period examples they too are.

The largest modern project has been restoring the old Customs House on the quayside to its glory of the 1760s, for this was an important port into the early 19th century and the building reflects it: just look at the portico, the stonework, the windows and the quoins - they all speak power, wealth and importance.

The various streets show off other Georgian and earlier properties, and there is space only to mention a few.

From the M6 the things which strike you are the
vast Moor hospital, formerly the mental asylum for the
whole county and dating from 1816 (though mainly
Victorian and later now), and the towering Ashton Memorial
in the superb Williamson Park. This memorial is 220 feet
high, a collossal domed pile of the 1900s designed by
John Belcher and which cost the unheard of sum of £87,000.
It was in memory of Lord Ashton's wife, he being the owner
of the local industrial giant. It stands on a hill and
one can get into to it and near the top thanks to recent
restoration work. Next door is the orangery, a butterfly
house but when I was a student it was an aviary. The whole
park and structure is magnificent, and only matched by
the views. Ashton (or Williamson as he began life) was the
linoleum king of the north, Liberal MP for the town,
and a local lad made good - his dad had a small oilcloth
business, and his son died in 1930 worth nearly £10,ooo,ooo.

One building actually about to fall down was the
Music Room near Market Street: it was in imminent danger in
1971 when I left, but on seeing it again in the 1980s I
was amazed at the beautiful restoration work by that
body known as the Landmark Trust to create a gem of which
any town would be proud. It had been a heavily plastered
and beautified graden room or pavilion in the garden of
Oliver Marton when built in the 1730s, but that garden
has now gone and it was left as an oasis of charm amidst
the buildings. There used to be others of the type, as in
Kendal up the road.

Of the churches mention needs to be made of
the Roman Catholic cathedral built in the late 1850s to
designs by Paley, and it sits near the middle of the vast
hill (lethal in frosty weather) up to the Ashton memorial.
It boasts a 240 foot tower and spire, a fine main church
and ancillary buildings, and good views. It dates of course
from the newfound confidence (and money) of the RC population
with the restoration of the Roman hierarchy in England,
and when their bishoprics could not be in places where
there was already an Anglican one. The district did have
many landowning RC families as well as the usual quota
of Irish.

There is just space to note the lovely Skerton
bridge coming into Lancaster from Morecambe which used to
be traffic jammed each morning (1780s and built for the
enormous sum of £14,000); the Judges' Lodgings, now a

museum, but a very fine 1620s town house taken over for
legal bodies and now a museum; the rather grand Storey
Institute of the 1880s given by the eponymous industrialist
of the city; and the delightful walks to be had within the
city centre and the outer suburbs, either following the
canal banks or other footpaths weaving round the main
streets.

St Martin's college occupies rising ground on an
excellent site going south of the town on the way to the
latest major source of employment, the university where I
was an undergraduate. This is now a very extensive
campus but still fairly isolated at Bailrigg and what
seemed like a day's journey in the dark of mornings or
evenings from October to March. It is something of a tourist
attraction, and like a small selfcontained town in its
own right.

Lancaster historically has enjoyed prosperity
from its legal position - any number of lawyers and
solicitors flourished there thanks to its county pre-eminence -
but it has also been a port which enjoyed considerable
medieval activity, a 16th and 17th century decline, and then
an 18th century flourish of trade with the Indies and
America. It is also world famous for having produced
outstanding furnitue thanks to Richard Gillow , using
the quality mahogany from the Indies for his 18th century
masterpieces (of which many remain in the town's
museums). Now Waring and Gillow, the firm remains
important for its furniture.

The town long had cotton and wool mills for
a variety of products including carpets, and the
importance of lionleum and allied products has been
mentioned. The Lancaster canal remains my favourite,
small yet in use, secluded yet known, though the stretch
in the city is not the nicest and used to have, when we
navigated it, a bad reputation on several counts as it
glides past mills and back lanes. The town too had
many firms connected with sailing boats and all their
needs from canvas to guns, though the advent of steam and
larger vessels in the 19th century more or less killed off
the port functions.

Historically Lancaster has enjoyed moderate
prosperity and lacked the boom-depression times of the
majority of larger and middling Lancashire towns: it was
never a place of reliance on a few staple trades or
industries, and all expansion or contraction was very
modest, not to say smallscale. It has an excellent social
and economic history published about itself as well as
many less academic books. The combination has made for
a fine county town: the past and present both in very good
condition ! And I should add, do not miss the canal's
brilliant aqueduct over the river Lune up river from the
town - one of Rennie's costing nearly £50,000, and
taking the canal majestically on five great arches for
hundreds of feet above the river.

SALFORD

Salford is not on the tourist beat, or at least
it never was till recently. I recall reading a book
of about 1950 by a local author describing what the many
bad points of Salford were (where he had been raised)
and how few the good ones were ! As a child we used to
go to see a distant relative once a year in the town,
and in the 1950s and 1960s the place was indeed full
of direst poverty, grime and all the accoutrements.
It was amongst the earliest recipients of a blaze of
publicity in the book written by Frederick Engels about
the industrial life of the 1840s: I, with my fellow
students, had to read it all in glorious detail.
Salford WAS the ultimate horror story of urban and
industrial Britain, but it has so changed in recent years
as to transform the whole scene. For a start it
has an ancient history and nowadays covers old centres
such as Worsley, Irlam and Eccles. It enjoys a very
fine museum and art gallery with a collection of L S
Lowry's paintings and recreation of streets and the
way the place was. The old and run down portside district
is now up and coming from redevelopment on the grand
scale, and much work has been done to improve the
many canal miles within the district. One never quite
gets over the shock of the water colour on the
Bridgewater canal at Worsley !

Good buildings are being cared for and put to
use too. Ordsall hall is a museum and a timber framed
house of the best quality; the old fire station, in
brashest brick, is a photographic centre and much loved;

The medieval and later Monks hall is also a museum,
another timber framed old property. This is new; so too
is the working class museum and library accumulated
by the Frows for many years in their house and now in
the Crescent: a unique archive celebrating working
class life and culture and the best collection of
relevant books in the country. One of Sir Charles
Barry's early buildings is a museum of mining on
Eccles Old Road: this, like all of the museums and
art galleries, is a must for the tourist.

The new university has been in the forefront of
the new Salford, but its modern buildings have a good
contrast with the cared for older ones and especially
the churches. It is a Roman Catholic diocese and the
HQ is an 1840s church much extended. A good Classical
design was employed for Smirke's St Phillip; whilst,
strange to say, there is a Greek church (Orthodox
Church) on Bury New Road and built for what was a
considerable Greek community c1860 !

An historic town ? Very much so.

MANCHESTER

How does one start to write just a handful of
pages about one of the best known of British cities,
which with its history, its industry and commerce, its
culture and sport, has become one of a few English
towns known around the globe ? Not easily. To start
with the town is big, both in population and in area,
and now more or less takes in many satellite towns
which until the 1950s were quite separate entities:
the resulting conurbation I have treated as so many
bits and pieces, so that Manchester alone is treated
herein.

For a start it occupies a place in literature.
Thomas De Quincey, the opium eating poet and writer,
was born here and attended Manchester grammar school
in the 1800s and ran away from it !   The famous
popularising novelist Harrison Ainsworth was a Manchester
lad, born in King Street in 1805 and also at the grammar
school: his novels have gone through many editions,
and Manchester figures in them. When any of our children
were dressed up beautifully by their granny we used to
call them a "Fauntleroy" - the creator of LITTLE LORD
FAUNTLEROY " and other books was Mrs Frances Hodgson
Burnett, who was born in Cheetham Hill Road in 1849
and lived in the worst part of Salford too before
emigrating to the USA and finding fame and fortune.
Of course Mrs Gaskell, Elizabeth Cleghorn as she was,
is the best known Mancunian by adoption: she married the

eminent Unitarian minister William Gaskell and spent her
entire married life in the town. Manchester was the
setting or inspiration for many of her books and
especially her first one MARY BARTON - though I must say
that the town fares rather badly ! She was about to
retire to leafy Hampshire when she dropped dead. One
whose books were also inspired by Manchester but which make
grim reading was Howard Spring, a journalist on the
MANCHESTER GUARDIAN 1915-1931: in similar vein
were the works of George Gissing, a student in the town
in the 1870s.

And so one could go on. But I must mention
the libraries: Chetham's library of the 1650s is
the oldest public one in the nation. The Portico
was the haunt of many literary lions. The enormous
John Rylands library on Deansgate is a vast monument
of the 1890s to the eponymous benefactor, and the place
is truly magnificent: I have used it on a number of
occasions and can recommend it to sightseers: enormous
hall, stairs, library and reading areas, superb original
light and toilet fitting (!) and so forth. A real
experience. It is of course a famous research place,
and I needed the best references to get in !

Manchester's history is as an important town
since Roman times and maybe earlier. The old history books
are full of the Roman inheritance, and of the Anglo-
Saxon one, but not much for any of these earlier epochs
has survived thanks to successive generations and their
insatiable appetite for change. The principal monument
to the middle age wool prosperity of the town is the
cathedral, which was founded as a great collegiate
body in the 1420s: thereafter the rector and members
of the college staff were about the best paid in the
county thanks to their vast tithes (which in truth
created enormous disputes later). Manchester tended
to be strongly parliamentarian and puritan in the
17th century, and the town was an important anti-
royalist centre both regionally and nationwide.
It was also of prominence in the Jacobite affairs of
1715 and 1746, though it was the 1640s which had brought
damaged property.

77

Population-wise there have been major changes
in the last 300 years, as might be expected. The town
of Manchester had about 23,000 inhabitants in 1774,
Salford about 5,000, but the actual parish was over
41,000 including the townships. By the first national
census of 1801 there had been a staggering increase to
71,000 for Manchester itself but over 102,000 for the whole
parish: by 1821 this was respectively 108,000 and
187,000. Through the Victorian years the population
swelled into the many hundreds of thousands, making it
the main town in a county of Victorian towns.

Rapid growth thanks to cotton and other
industries led to slums and to social problems on a
scale only equalled in 3 or 4 major British cities.
Manchester was also a radical political centre: the
newly rich Manchester manufacturers were to the fore
in political reform debates from the 1790s and were
rewarded by their own MPs in 1832. But below them lay
others of inferior social rank who wanted power: hence
the mobs, the riots, Peterloo in 1819 when so many were
killed at a mass meeting, the Blanketeers, the Luddites,
the Chartists and others who spanned 1800 to 1850.
Thereafter developments were more peaceful, as society was
more prosperous. The population and suburbs expanded
regardless, and Cheshire was early invaded. Today
most of east Cheshire is the new suburb of Manchester.

There is only time and space in passing to
mention such things as the canals and then the great
ship canal of the 1880s, the railway revolution,
civic and public developments, the hundreds of places of
worship, the charities and societies to help all type
of person (and creature), the schools and university
and their origins, the enormous Sunday schools and
religious life, the newspapers, political and economic
developments, arts and so on. One could write a book on a small
part of Manchester: any directory of Lancashire is
packed with the history and life of Manchester, and
even more so than of the great arch rival Liverpool.

Architecturally there are many jewels which
are worth looking at.

78

First the cathedral, elevated from great parish church in 1847, and more or less a vast Perpendicular building with choir rebuilt c1430 and the nave c1470. The tower was in turn heightened and rebuilt in the 1860s, and the arcades in the 1880s, but all in the old style. A fair amount of work such as chapels, vestries and porches were later added or made new, to give an almost square main building. I always find it rather gloomy inside, a bit like Westminster abbey, but there is no denying its quality.

At the other extreme is Fletcher Moss gallery and museum, which is in Didsbury and a very pleasant 19th century parsonage now finding a new role. Platt Hall in Rusholme is a grander Georgian country house and housing a museum of English costume. At Prestwich is Heaton Hall, a very large neo-Classical mansion and filled with period furniture and the like. Rather more modest is Wythenshaw Hall in Northenden, a Tudor manor house of distinction and the home of the Tattons for centuries. This too is a museum and displaying its own history. And not forgetting that woman, Mrs Pankhurst, her home at Nelson Street is a good example of Georgian villas, and now a centre with displays of the WSPU and the family which achieved so much through their struggle in the 1900s.

The Manchester museum housed at the university on Oxford Road (to which I once made the mistake of walking from the cathedral in August) houses an important scientific and natural history exhibition. There are some strange little museums - like those at the Manchester United football club premises, and the "museum" at Granada TV for CORONATION STREET. Far larger is the museum of science and industry near Deansgate: smaller is the Jewish museum on Cheetham Hill Road.

I can remember the Jewish quarter of the city - strange to say, and the Chinatown - but we never stopped off in either! It speaks volumes for the sheer size and cosmopolitan quality of the town that Manchester could support two such dissimilar communities for so long. There are others: the Moravian community has a delightful quarter, well worth a visit.   To those who do not know, these were the people who so impressed the Wesleys on their way to America, but whose religious history departed shortly afterwards from those two founding Methodists.

79

Manchester town centre seems so much bigger than Liverpool. The Central library for example is huge, a purpose built building actually opened by the king and queen in the 1930s and having the distinction of being one of the largest in the world. Not far away from it is the larger than life town hall by local architect Alfred Waterhouse. This building was opened in 1877 and took a million pounds and nine years to construct, being one of the grandest of its kind and one of the largest ever designs by an architect on a single edifice. It is the scale which impresses, all in Victorian Gothic, and with nearly 300 foot of tower in the middle - and what about the set of state rooms inside, or the sculptures, or the Pre-Raphaelite murals ?

Queen Victoria's husband, Albert, was a great fan of the energetic Manchester Men, so that on his death in 1861 the town did him proud by commissioning Thomas Worthington to design a fitting memorial. This large monument, the Albert Memorial (what else !) was apparently copied by Sir George Scott in London - I remember there being rows about it in the press of the day since Scott claimed it all as his.

The town centre has its statues too including a big one of President Lincoln of the USA in recognition of the support given by the town to the North against the slavery state of the South in the 1860s - the socalled Cotton Famine caused untold hardship for Lancashire people since no cotton could be imported. The Free Trade Hall (named after the fight to end protectionism which hindered trade) is another grand building, home to the Halle orchestra.

The present countycourt was home to the leader of political reform, Richard Cobden, and after his day it was the first home for Owens college which in turn developed into the present university: quite a pedigree ! Not that far away is St Anne's church of the 1700s, a rare Wren-style building for the district and lovely. A pity that more of the city of that type and date have not survived. In the square stands the Royal Exchange building , now a theatre, but once packed out with thousands of cotton merchants and others transacting their business.

80

Near the cathedral is Chetham's Hospital school
and library housed in the substantial town house of the
De La Warre family, and a house of 1100 rebuilt in the
15th century as home for the college of priests. After
the Civil Wars it was home to the Derbys who seem to have
added the 17th century interior, and eventually that
century the famous school.

One could go on for reams about the other
buildings, so many of them Victorian and later but all
noteworthy architectural efforts, and often involved in
commercial and business life from the start. The banks
and their premises could take a whole book ! There
are masses of shops, covered areas and arcades for
shopping, Arndale and other centres all catering for
hordes of out of town shoppers or city centre workers
and dedicated to their entertainment and money-relieving
facilities !

So what does Manchester historically mean to
visitors ? Well it is all a matter of one's own
experiences. For me, it is the libraries and the
museums (inevitably) but also the gigantic inflatable
Father Christmas tied to the town hall clock tower;
exquisite luncheons at the Sawyer's Arms or Sinclair's
bar; the array of goods in Kendal Milne's shops; the
enormous railway station at rush hour; a quiet sandwich
in St Anne's Square with the flowers and pigeons for
company. And those washrooms at the Rylands !

81

LIVERPOOL

Liverpool is one of the major cities of Britain
and of Europe, actually better known than most simply
due to its popular music of the 1960s. There was a
smallsettlement here in Domesday of the 1080s and 100
or so habitations in the 13th century alongside a small
castle (which went forever in the 1720s). There
were a number of rather better houses put up in the
16th century when Elizabethan gentry found it handy to
have a town house, including the Stanleys who owned
Knowsley, not that far inland.   These too went in
the generally total rebuilding of the city in the 19th
century, and again in the total redevelopment of huge
areas of what had become a major port and city in the
20th.

Liverpool was a small port serving local
county needs in the 16th century, and caught up to
some extent in the developing Irish and American
trades - but in a very small way. The big local families
were the Stanley earls of Derby and the Molineux earls
of Sefton; what changed things was, firstly the granting
of a town charter in the 1620s to a new corporation which
could then develop the town, and secondly the important
role played by the port in the parliamentary interest
against the king during the Civil Wars.

82

Despite the increasing importance of the port
in the 1640s, reports c1650 indicate that there were only
15 or 20 ships attached to it and nothing over 35 tons,
and in Daniel Defoe's day, c1700, passengers were
still forced to be carried from boats in the water on
the backs of local yokels ! The town was only made
into a separate parish about 1699, ironically carved out
of ancient Walton itself now simply a small part of the
city. That was also the year in which a dock was at last
built for vessels, and growth remained slow of both town
and port. During the 1700s Chester more or less shut
down as a serious port, and with the accelerating Irish
and new slave trade growth, the port started to take
off as the century progressed.

With each decade population, vessels numbers
and tonnage, trade and industry increased, and especially
so after 1746 and the final settling of the Jacobite
business. The population is hard to determine due to
parochial confusion, but the actual town of Liverpool
appears to have had 5,000 inhabitants about 1700;
12,000 in 1720; 18,000 in 1750; and 34,000 in 1770.
By the first census of 1801 it was a staggering 77,000
and 118,000 at the census of 1821. By that date too
something around 6,000 ships were berthing and loading or
unloading or both in Liverpool. The docks were successively
rebuilt or added to in number, and alongside these grew
up hundreds of acres of ancillary accommodation in the
form of offices, bays, warehouses and yards. With the
course of the Victorian decades this was increasingly the
case, providing mile after mile of dockland.

With such rampant economic activity, and
always centred on the port and its myriad functions, came
a host of charitable, benevolent and educational
societies and institutions, vast numbers of schools and
above all churches and chapels, and a whole new range of
public buildings ranging from rebuilt town halls and
business exchanges to hospitals and almshouses. One
can only guess at the numbers involved in building the
great new town and its docks. Well known industries in
Liverpool of c1820 included pottery and china, salt
and sugar refining, malting and brewing, iron foundries
and metal trades, precision instruments including
clocks and watches. A rich diversity only added to by
the port business.

A Philosophical and Literary society, several
considerable libraries and newsrooms, 7 weekly newspapers,
theatre, music hall, circus, racecourse, Botanic gardens,
Athenaeum, Lyceum, Royal Institution and similar
bodies were all active c1800 and show the wealth of
a booming provincial town. The sudden influx of Irish
Roman Catholics from the 1800s, and escalating into a
deluge in the 1840s when famine struck Ireland,
added a new pressure to the growing population - hence the
warring bands of Irish RCs versus Orangemen ever since.
As the 19th century progressed came the railways which
quickly crushed the slow and inflexible canal system;
the docks and port expanded ever increasingly; the hinter-
land on wich the port could draw stretched through Cheshire
and to Manchester and the Pennines; and the urban
district, thanks to the work of scores of speculative
builders, took over the host of villages and hamlets
which were once (and certainly before 1830) idyllically
rural - Everton, Walton, Bootle, Wavertree and Allerton
for instance. Before the century was out, even the
remoteness of Knowsley, the Derby family seat, was linked
to Liverpool on one side and to Prescot and St Helens
on the other. Today there is nothing but townscape.

It is impossible in so small a space to do justice
to the whole gamut of a large city's history, or of
its buildings. In the following lines are details on
some of the items not to be missed in this fine and
cosmopolitan place.

The view that one remembers from the sea
is of the three buildings, the Royal Liver , the
Cunard, and the Port of Liverpool: world famous and
splendid, all quite different and of varying roof
details and heights. And what about St George's hall,
scene of so many concerts and similar, or the town hall,
enormous and awe-inspiring ? Areas and streets of interest
abound even after so many merciless developments:
Rodney and Water Streets, Grassendale and Childwall,
Princes Park and Sunnyside, Percy Street and Gambier
Terrace, Bold Street and all the others: all different,
all fascinating, and scenes of endless human activity.

Museum-wise the city too is rich. The Liverpool
Museum in William Brown Street possesses collections of

national and world interest. The Museum of Labour History
in Islington is housed in the old county sessions house,
and covers such aspects as the various jobs and trades
of the district, housing and schools, the unions and
so on. And Albert Dock ! What a transformation in
recent years from the wasteland which it had become.
It is seen daily on TV, and contains the Maritime museum
which shows off the proud heritage of what was once the
second port of the nation. It also has a number of
actual ships and vessels to explore: it takes hours to
get round thoroughly.

The art galleries were our haunts as 5th
and 6th formers: we were dragged round them, unappreciative
of either the Walker in William Brown Street or of any
other gallery: but the Walker is world renowned, and was
awash with old masters from Europe, from memory.

Further out of town is Speke Hall, which
I was taken to aged 10 with a school party to find out
about the 16th century: what we found was one of those
rare survivals, a complete Elizabethan house, full of
priest holes and other delicious secrets which cast a
spell over visitors. Back into the town and what about
the places of worship ? Rivalry for centuries between
Anglican and Roman Catholic has produced a city of
exceptional religious vitality. The RC cathedral was
the centre of attraction for all Lancashire in the 1960s
and is as startlingly modern as the gigantic Anglican
one is anachronistic. The latter took nearly a
century to build, the largest Gothic building in the
country, and has just been finished. Its vast tower
rises above the city from all directions, and it is built
on a mound which was a rubbish tip from the old quarry
of the 1760s which gave work to city unemployed. Just
stand and gape at the glass, the stone, the arches,
the tremendously inspiring ensemble. A giant .

Smaller churches impress: a whole clan of
Nonconformist ones from the riches of 18th and 19th
century Dissenting communities. The Anglicans have
the gaunt shell of St Luke's in Leece Street to remind of
war bombing, plus the sailors' church of Our Lady and
St Nicholas, and the first iron church in the world,
St George's at Everton (and dated 1814).

Liverpool has historically enjoyed some fine
parks, including a number of gardens in the centres of
squares. Sefton is the star, 270 acres with considerable
glass houses and lake. Calderstones is smaller and
more selective in its exhibits of trees. We used to have
a day out to Otterspool promenade and the socalled
linear park, a long narrow strip which follows alongside
the river Mersey - but the water never looked inviting,
and always grey !

We used to go to Liverpool to savour the excitement of Bold Street shopping, to find clothes to fit us all
at the outsize shops (!we are all vast!), to see the best
street markets available (including John Street pets,
however callous it now seems) and to drink in the big city
atmosphere that has created the Clayton Square shopping
centre for a staggering £40 million, or the £10 million
St John's centre. Liverpool shows up on TV in many
programmes, often comedy ones: I should imagine they
are very popular down the Mersey way. Historically it
remains a fascinating city, at its best in or near the
centre, though it is far too extensive to allow for
short walks or easy stages - all is on the grand size,
both history and the architecture.

It would be easy to note the musical talent
in the city of Liverpool, but less well known is
the number of literary connections. Shakespeare is the
earliest since it is generally believed that he was
performing at Knowlsey for the Stanleys c1590 - but never
fully proved of course ! When the town was all port
and surrounding villages, the great essayist William
Hazlitt stayed locally for some time; so too did
Thomas De Quincey, later one of the Lake Poets in the
circle surrounding the Wordsworths, and both c1790-1800.
I recall my grandparents having a library stocked
with the works of Felicia Hemans, who was raised in the
town in the 1790s as Miss Brown and achieved fame as
poet and novelist but not in Liverpool.

Charles Dickens visited Liverpool on a number
of occasions from the 1830s, giving readings and acting
in the theatre on some trips. Phiz, that is Hablot
Browne who illustrated for Boz, that is early Dickens,
had a son practising in Rodney Street. Dickens gave
many references to the town in his articles and
novels, but he did not enjoy the claim to fame of

86

Mathew Arnold, the poet and author who dropped dead
in the port whilst awaiting the return of his daughter
from the USA in 1888. And so the list of literary
worthies might be added to, and most of them in the
19th century went to Liverpool. I might mention in
passing that from my own studies I came across two
men with Liverpool links. One was Sir James Frazer,
who wrote the mammoth set of volumes THE GOLDEN BOUGH,
which is just about the definitive work on magic,
superstition and folklore round the world.   He
was professor of social anthropology at Liverpool
university from the 1900s to the 1920s - that hater
of the Victorian way of life, Lytton Strachey, was an
undergraduate in the city in the 1890s before he
put pen to paper. And finally A C Bradley, another
whose copious volumes I worked upon, was the first
professor of English Literature and history at the
city's university in the 1880s - his criticisms
and commentaries on Shakespeare are still the standard
works on the theme, and brilliant.

87

CLITHEROE   and   WHALLEY

      Often featured for its many picturesque and
charming qualities, Clitheroe is one of the most user-
friendly of all towns in the county - even the excellent
car parking facilities are free ! How irksome to have to
pay to park ! It remains small, and was an ancient borough
for centuries. Its most characteristic view is of the
castle, a small Norman keep and various remains perched
on a big lump of limestone, gently masked by trees from
some angles and with the ring of various medieval and
Georgian properties, rather like Durham but far, far
smaller and more modest.

      Historically the town into the 19th century was
under the vast parish of Whalley but it enjoyed the
wide variety of occupations to be found in all the small
market towns. The industrial revolution simply brought
a few extra jobs and mainly in cotton mills - printing
the cotton, spinning, weaving and so on, with the river
Ribble and its streams providing the power along with an
array of steam engines.

      The main historic building is the castle,
with its keep only 35 foot square. The main parish church
of St Mary Magdalene is medieval but drastically rebuilt
by Rickman in the 1820s (as so many were). Still it has
atmosphere and is something of a tourist attraction.
Rickman also built the town hall which was later added
to. Several mills remain - above all Low Moor, which is
a sort of mill settlement with several hundred terraced

houses by it. The settlement originated with a Mr Jackson
but it shortly came under Garnett and Horsfalls.

Whalley should be mentioned for its ancient
importance. In 1801 it was head of a parish of
50,000 people, including 13 chapelries and 48 townships
- 1 borough and 4 market towns. Yet less than 900
lived actually in Whalley town. It had the usual history
of villages with its crafts and small businesses, some
cotton working, and not much else. However there is
an especially important parish church (of St Mary)
and the abbey ruins.

St Mary's contains Norman and medieval work
including big tower, sedilia and piscina, superb choir
stalls of the 15th century taken from the abbey down
the road, and a wealth of fitments and furnishings of
note - chandeliers, screens, pews, monuments, glass,
organ case.

The abbey is most unusual, a very late
Cistercian foundation of the 1290s after they had been
forced off their Cheshire site by flooding. PLenty of
remains too for the tourists, including massive gateway,
abbot's lodging, part of the cloisters, arches.
The abbey church was 260 feet, average size only, for the
Cistercians when one thinks of Fountains and Rievaulx.
The Order was austere, eschewing decoration and the frills
and frippery associated with many Orders. The abbey was
often in legal wrangles with other Houses and bishops over
income and finance, which bled its resources for centuries:
but it remained an important house.

Whalley has a number of satisfying houses and
cottages of both brick and stone. It figured in the
researches and writings of the Lancashire novelist
Harrison Ainsworth in the early Victorian years as he
publicised such episodes in the history of the county as
the Lancashire witches.

Whalley and Clitheroe are the two centres for
much of the lovely Ribble valley. Many will know the district
because of the novel THE LANCASHIRE WITCHES, which
vividly portrays the early 17th century doings of those
poor unfortunates who ended up hanged at Lancaster in so
many instances. What a load of rubbish too was written

and spoken of witchcraft, especially round Sabden and
Pendle district. The many villages however invite
inspection though they fall outside the scope of this
book.

I include in this section a brief mention of
Stonyhurst, a famous public school forming a triangle
corner with the two towns. It was a medieval house
that seems to have been rebuilt in Tudor times, replaced
in the 1590s and 1600s with a new mansion, when it was
the home of the Shireburns. It was neglected in the way
that many mansions were by impoverished RC owners in the
18th century, and home to the duchess of Norfolk (a
daughter of the Shireburns and married into the greatest
RC family of the nation). Eventually it was given by
a new owner called Weld to the Society of Jesus in the
1790s, a body in disarray on the continent thanks to the
wars and repression.

The new school replaced the old English RC
college at Douai, and throughout the 19th and 20th
centuries it has expanded remorselessly . Extentions in
1799, a big church of the 1830s after the passing of
the emancipation act let RCs into many previously barred
aspects of public life, continuous work in the 1840s
and 1850s, and in the 1870s and 1880s, and more this century.
It might well become a tourist attraction itself one
day !

LEIGH

have been a number of similar losses.

        The various chapelries and townships are
more or less one, joined up by 150 years of
urbanisation and industrialisation. The directories
before 1830 list farmers by the score for this quite
small parish (only 12,000 acres), but the seed
for growth was already apparent in the many metal
trades at work, plus a few small mills and a handful
of coal mine owners. The landscape and townscape has
altered more hereabouts than anywhere in the district.

        As a child I was often taken through Leigh on
the way to somewhere, but never to Leigh itself because
it was regarded as inferior to both Wigan and St Helens
in every way. I noticed the other day that it was one of
the few places too without much in the way of tourist
information available. Sadly it is one of those
places which, judging by early directories, was far more
attractive in 1820 than it has been this century,
mainly thanks to the Victorian inheritance of vast
numbers of terraced houses, blackened with muck.
It is an ancient market town but one would never
have guessed it, and has long been involved with the
coal trade from whence the people gained their
income. It also sits on a junction of the duke of
Bridgewater's canal with the Leeds Liverpool, which
was especially helpful for transporting all goods
and passengers before the railways arrived in the
1830s.

        Into the 1820s Leigh remained only a place with
 2,000 inhabitants, though its parish, covering Astley,
Atherton, Tyldesley, Bedford and Pennington had 18,000
by 1831. All was to explode in size thanks to coal,
the railways and allied changes. From the descriptions
of the place before 1830 one would not now recognise
any part of it. One must regret the loss of so many
good buildings including the hall built by the
Atherton family in the 1700s which was ruinous in the
early 19th and knocked down. It was one of the most
splendid of the county, so descriptions go, there

BLACKPOOL

Blackpool today is one of the greatest of
British seaside resorts, epitomising what people
want in the way of fun, excitement, pleasure and
activity, and enormously popular with millions visiting
it each year. In the mid 18th century it was frequented
by a small gentried elite from the county who found its
bathing more beneficial, more convenient and cheaper
than pleasures in Bath or elsewhere: its population
in the 1820s had grown to 750 plus visitors, but
when I first knew it in the 1960s it had become a big
town of over 150,000 people: a revolution indeed.

Its parent parish was little Bispham with
Norbreck, which included Layton with Warbreck and
had a population of about 1,000 in the 1820s - now
it is entirely integrated in Blackpool and known more
or less from hotel names. Descriptions of what the
whole place was like before the Victorians are not
really believable: the whole unspoilt coastline,
nothing but farms and cottages and a Norman church
demolished in the 1880s.

Blackpool slowly grew, rather like Southport,
throughout the early 19th century: the whole pace of
change rocketed with the arrival of the railway in
1846 and attendant workers, and above all after
1860 - it was the combination of more leisure time with
more money, with aspirations and desires, and the proximity
of the town to the main Lancashire industrial districts
which led to the Victorian boom. Even so, there is
not much in the way of pre-1870s buildings to see,
just occasional bits and pieces and the overall
impression is of post 1900 in every direction with
odd major exceptions. The shopping centre and
shopping streets seem enormous , for instance, and
the promenade is not only vastly long but hugely wide
in many places.

The social and economic history of Blackpool
has already been written. Suffice it to say that the
town earns its living from tourism and the services needed
for them and the workers. The town is architecturally
poor: dozens of Victorian and modern churches and public
buildings but not much else. Not that money was not
spent on architecture, but as has been said in many
places, taste was lacking.

St John, All Hallows, Sacred Heart and others
are typical Blackpool churches; the town hall is
as one would expect, brick and big. The star is the
tower (with its assorted delights !) which rises a
massive 500 feet above the countryside. It is a
conscious copy of the Eiffel tower in Paris but about
half the size. To ascend it is an experience, and before
modern developments in highrise it was a thrilling
landmark.

The Winter gardens were vastly expensive -
vulgar and tasteless many said - they cost hundreds of
thousands of pounds in the 1870s and 1890s when they
were built, along with their pavilion and opera house.
The hotels too show well what the town is: the
Norbreck, Carlton, Imperial, clifton and scores of
oters. These have always been for the elite, the
rabble making do with some thousands of back street
guest houses and more modern middling hotels !

The original bathing was carried out from
conveyances drawn into the sea or as near to it as possible:
the ladies emerged in their costumes after the ringing
of a bell told the gents to stay away, and another bell
signalled when they might approach. Men who did not obey
this unwritten rule of conduct forfeited their reputation
and a bottle of wine to the company !

In the late 1820s the principal hotels were Banks', Gaskells' and Dixon's, and these charged 5 or 6shillings per night per person, with extra for front rooms with a view. The cheapest hotel seems to have charged half a crown (2s 6d) per night, and then the humbler classes had to go to a boarding or lodging establishment of which there were a dozen to choose from. It was all very hierarchical and very structured, and entertainments were decidedly restricted: drinking in the pubs or hotels, occasional guest troupes of actors and the like, a coffeeroom, newsroom and library. Plenty of cardplaying and occasional dances and balls at the three main hotels.

One can scarcely believe that the vast array of amusements and entertainments along the golden mile have not always been there ! Should one wish to see how Blackpool more or less looked in 1820, then I can recommend a visit to Allonby in West Cumberland, which is a totally stunted place just as Blackpool must have been in 1820 - it makes fascinating contrast.

CHORLEY

Chorley is one of the nicest of industrial towns and has a long history as market centre for a wide area. Nature has provided the hills so necessary to good town development; there are views, a good centre, a sea of new development, and excellent roads. Early directories speak of the wealth of the town via its deposits of coal, lime, lead and other ores, its waterpower and quarrying . The population was a healthy 4,500 in 1801 and had about doubled 30 years later thanks to industrial and manufacturing activity.

Architecturally there are some notable buildings. The parish church of St Laurence is big and medieval, but suffered a great restoration in the 1850s so common in the country. The interior offers woodwork and monuments to local worthies. The Church Commissioners financed a new church of St George, in the 1820s and it cost over £12,000; designed by Thomas Rickman (the former druggist, painter and surgeon turned architect, who also invented the inadequate architectural language still in use) it is a good late Georgian design with above all much room for the congregation - which was the whole point of the exercise - in generous galleries. It was asserted at the time that 2,000 worshippers could be comfortably accommodated within St George's: were there ever that many one wonders ?

Chorley, as might be expected, furnished
a rich diversity of churches: fine Unitarian, RC,
Methodist, and Congregational chapels in the later
18th or early 19th centuries, often extended or rebuilt
in the Victorian era. Schools too, both day and
Sunday ones, struggled to cope with the rising number
of youngsters, who formed 40 to 50% of the total
population in many years . It was a very youthful
population partly due to the high birth rate and
high death rate !

The Victorian town hall replaced what was
described as a model building of 1802 and paid for
by John Hollinshead of the town. It was the common
type of arrangement, with large business or meeting
room for the council or JPs upstairs, small lock
up and open columned area beneath for market and
traders throughout the week.

The outstanding building in Chorley attracts
visitors by the thousand: Astley Hall.

The mansion of the Charnock family in the
15th century, Astley hall was rebuilt c1600 into a
grand Elizabethan country house, which was then
substantially rebuilt in the mid 17th century to add
to the puzzle. Just look at the glass, the plasterwork
and woodwork inside ! Well worth a walk to view it
both as home and as museum and gallery.

Finally one would not view Chorley as social
pacesetter: yet it enjoyed a reservoir and fresh supply
of piped water from about 1823, gas provision
from 1819, and a number of small (and limited)
building societies in self-help mood which provided
hundreds of houses for their participants. Of course
these were not the grand financial bodies we now
have, but simple mutual aid ones for the members to
be helped in their homebuilding. In Chorley it
worked. How many of the increasing number of
cotton and silk mill workers lived in mill houses
I do not know, and they were probably just a bit too
poor to afford the wages of the skilled elite of
artisans who joined the societies.

LYTHAM ST ANNES

So united are these two separate settlements
that they are always dealt with together, but if one
visits them, their differing history, buildings and
feel are quite evident. Lytham is the older part,
an ancient parish with market place, hall and the
trappings of heritage altered by growth into a resort.
St Annes is somewhat brasher, newer, a suburb of
the Fylde coast holiday extravaganza of the Victorian
and later years.

Early directories said that if the elite
went to Blackpool in the 1820s and earlier, almost as
respectable a lot attended Lytham and in greater
numbers. According to Baines' directory, the landowner
refused to grant long leases, so that outsiders would
not hazard building the villas and buildings so requisite
for material advance and prosperity; and they also had
to obtain permission off the landowner to resell. The
landowners were the Cliftons of Lytham hall, who also
enjoyed the main river pool on the river Ribble and
its estuary, a mile from the town, which was the main
unloading and loading point for Preston. So the little
town was something of a port too, but there was
no chance of wharves, piers and harbour thanks to the
restricted landholding conditions still in use.

Bearing in mind that three coaches only arrived
with tourists each day in the summer season at Lytham,
and all from Preston, the restricted nature of the

tourist trade in Lytham in the 1820s can be gauged.
The resident population was about 1300 at that time.

Architecturally there are some gems to view,
though so many of the old, thatched and picturesque
cottages and houses have long gone.

The old hall was a 17th century manor with
high chimneystacks, gables and mullioned windows -
a real 1600s Lancashire house. The Cliftons called
in the eminent architect John Carr of York to provide
a more fitting mansion, which he duly did at great
cost. Today that house is the showpiece of the town,
bright brick, 9 bays long and 5 wide, and distinctive
Gibbs windows. Gibbs decorations are matched with
Adam style ones, hence the fine plaster ceilings and
decorations.

The parish church of Lytham is St Cuthbert's
an 1830s building which replaced one of the 1760s,
but itself much changed and enlarged. When I stayed at
Lytham some years ago I had the chance to observe
the other places of worship including a most showy
Methodist church, RC, Congregational and others.
The town hall is one of those 1920s Classical attempts
to match the hall. Rather nicer are the older houses,
especially places like Bath Street, Dicconson Terrace,
the Market Square and others. On the very pleasant
seafront and green is the famous windmill - an eyecatcher
for all the visitors.

St Annes, uncomfortably sandwiched between
giant Blackpool and genteel Lytham, grew after the
railway brought in the trippers in the late 1840s,
but mostly after increasing leisure and incomes and
bank holidays from the 1870s.

One or two cottages and houses apart, and
these are outposts of old Lytham, St Annes wears the
guise of tourism and settlement after 1870, and above
all 1890-1910 : bargeboarding and massive steep gables
everywhere, beloved by speculative builders but a
nightmare to maintain today.

There is the usual crop of parish and Dissenting
churches: St Anne's itself, an 1870s parish church .

Drawn by R. Carlyle.   On Zinc by L. Haghe.   Printed from Zinc by Day & Haghe.

FURNESS ABBEY,
from the West.

Published by D. Atkinson, Ulverston.

Drawn by R. Carlyle.   On Zinc by L. Haghe.   Printed from Zinc by Day & Haghe.

FURNESS ABBEY,
from the West.

Published by D. Atkinson, Ulverston.

Engraved by J.T.Willmore.

SOUTH EAST VIEW,

OF FURNESS ABBEY.

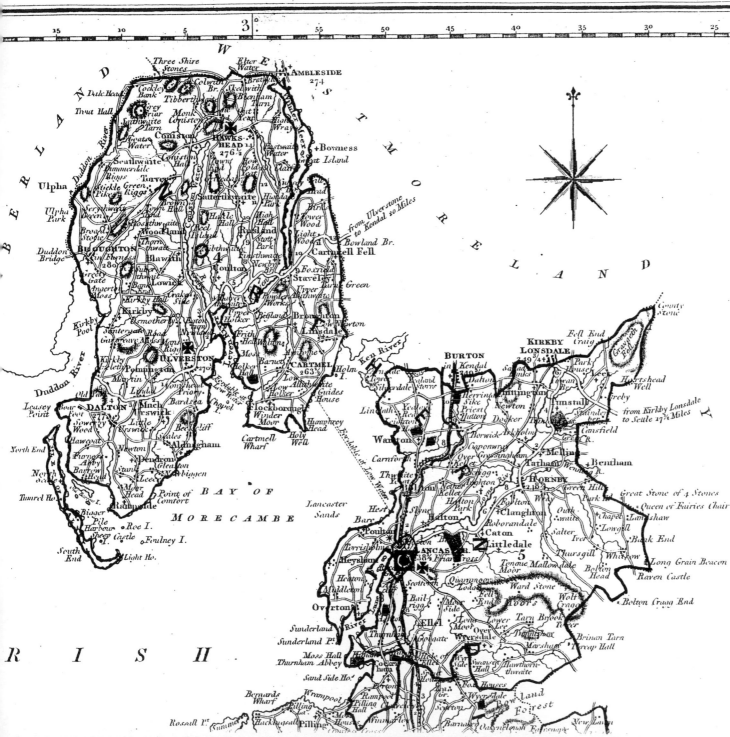

LANCASHIRE.

EXPLANATION.

Market Towns with the distance from London in measured Miles as........ } ROCH...

Churches and Chapels _ _ _ _ _ _ _

Turnpike Roads _ _ _ _ _   Mail Co...

Bye Roads _ _ _ _ _ _ _

Navigable Canals _ _ _ _ _ _ _

Rivers _ _ _ _ _ _ _

Seats of the Nobility and Gentry _ _ _ _

N.B. The figures on the Turnpike Roads shew th distance in measured Miles between the Towns.

Railways _ _ _ _ _ _ _

Population Nth Divn 343,373 Assessd Taxes £
Do   Sth Divn 993,119   Do   Do £

ILLUSTRATIONS

Photographs of c1920
Prints of the Victorian years

Engraved by J.T.Willmore.

SOUTH EAST VIEW,

OF FURNESS ABBEY.

Drawn by R. Carlyle.　　On Zinc by L. Haghe.　　Printed from Zinc by Day & Haghe.

FURNESS ABBEY,
from the West.

Published by D. Atkinson, Ulverston.

Drawn by R Carlyle

VIEW OF FURNESS ABBEY.
from the School House.

Printed from Stone by Day & Hagh

Published by D. Atkinson, Ulverston.

Drawn by R. Carlyle. On Zinc by L. Haghe. Printed from Zinc by Day & Haghe.

FURNESS ABBEY,
from the West.

Published by D. Atkinson, Ulverston.

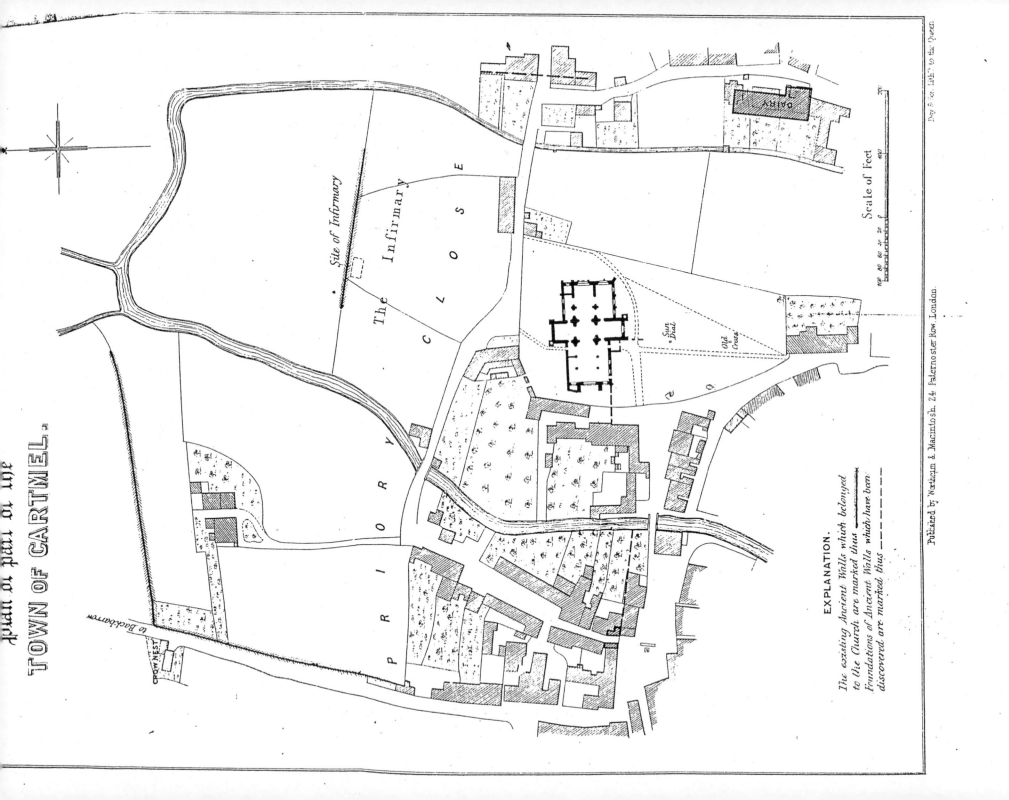

Plan or part of the

TOWN OF CARTMEL.

to Backbarrow

CROW NEST

P R I O R Y

T h e   C L O S E

The Infirmary

Site of Infirmary

Sun Dial

Old Cross

DAIRY

EXPLANATION.

The existing Ancient Walls which belonged
to the Church are marked thus
Foundations of Ancient Walls which have been
discovered are marked thus

Scale of Feet

Published by Warkam & Macintosh, 24 Paternoster Row London.

Day & Son. Lith.rs to the Queen.

CARTMEL 1877

CARTMEL CHURCH.

VIEW of FURNESS ABBEY from the SOUTH WEST.

Dixo 1-Scott

THROUGH MANCHESTER THE ROAD TO GLASGOW GOES ON TO PRESTON

Piccadilly, in Manchester, is a continuation of the London Road, and the open space to one side of it, formerly occupied by an infirmary, is the site of the new art gallery and museum. Preston (top) possesses an imposing set of buildings in its market-place. These include, besides the town hall, the great building of the Harris Free Public Library and Museum, built after a Greek style by James Hilbert, in 1893. Next to it, on the left, is the Sessions Hall, with a tower which is 179 feet tall. Preston boasts some of the finest public buildings in the country.

Scott

Annan

TYNE, CLYDE AND MERSEY, WHOSE MOUTHS MAKE THREE OF BRITAIN'S GREATEST PORTS

South Shields (bottom left) stands on the right bank of the Tyne at its mouth and opposite North Shields. The name derives from the shiels or fishermen's huts, at the river mouth, which made the beginnings of a great port. The shipping of coal is its chief business. Along the Broomielaw (bottom right), which lies beside the Clyde in the heart of Glasgow, is the steamboat quay whence the steamers run to Gourock, Wemyss Bay and Rothesay. Below the city the Clyde has some of the largest shipbuilding yards in the world. From the Mersey (top photographs) sail the ships for America. The huge structures (top right) along the river front are, from left to right, the Liver Building, the Cunard Building and the premises of the Dock Board.

L.M.S.

ULLSWATER FROM GOWBARROW PARK: CONISTON AND THE "OLD MAN"

Once known as Thurston Mere, the lake of Coniston (top) is noted for its wooded banks and islands. It is over five miles long and half a mile wide. Beyond it, on the east side, is the mountain called Coniston Old Man, whence the Welsh mountains round Snowdon can be descried in the right weather. It is 2,633 feet high. "The Old Man" is much disfigured by mines and quarries, and copper mines are said to have been worked in the district in Roman days. From the park of Gowbarrow Hall, on the north side of Ullswater, we get this fine view (bottom).

Dixon-Scott

Frith

CHESTER'S THIRTEENTH CENTURY CHOIR AND LIVERPOOL MAGNIFICENTLY NEW

We are looking from the choir of Chester's red sandstone cathedral (bottom) through the modern choir screen towards the West End. The stalls, which have fine spiral canopies, date from the close of the fourteenth century. Liverpool Cathedral (top) was begun in 1904 for the diocese created in 1880, the architect being Sir Giles Gilbert Scott. His designs were adopted when he was twenty-one. The style may be called a free interpretation of Gothic, and when complete this will be England's largest cathedral. The